Merline –

These photos remind me
so much of you & of all the
quiet, peaceful hours we have shared
in your garden. It is your generosity and
inspiration that makes me realize that
a garden is a place where "work"
& "celebration" become more & more a
single, continual experience.

Happy Birthday!

Love, Richard

open air living

open air living
creative ideas for stylish outdoor living

Enrica Stabile
photography by Christopher Drake

text by Alice Berkeley
step-by-step projects by Lucinda Ganderton and Mark Ripley

RYLAND
PETERS
& SMALL
London New York

To Elisabetta's memory, with whom I
shared so much and whom I miss so much.

Designer   Catherine Randy
Senior editor   Sophie Bevan
Location research   Enrica Stabile, Alice Berkeley
Production   Patricia Harrington
Art director   Gabriella Le Grazie
Publishing director   Alison Starling

Illustrations by Lizzie Sanders
Text by Alice Berkeley

First published in the USA in 2001
by Ryland Peters & Small, Inc.
519 Broadway, 5th Floor
New York, NY 10012
www.rylandpeters.com

ISBN 1 84172 158 1

A CIP catalog for this book is available from
the Library of Congress

Printed and bound in China

contents

introduction

The great outdoors is man's natural habitat. From the beginning, he sheltered under trees, bathed in rushing streams, and slept on mossy sod. He picked fruit from trees, fished for his supper, and crushed grapes to make wine. He clothed himself with woven grasses and cured leather, and built shelters from sticks and stones. The sun, rain, and wind were all part of daily life.

Our intellectual and artistic creativity, too, is traditionally kindled by contact with nature. Great open spaces give us a feeling of freedom and joy; in the woods, the garden, or by the sea, we see color, movement, and wildlife that stimulate our imagination and sense of the infinite.

This book is about expanding our indoor life to the outdoors—making outdoor activities a part of everyday existence. It explores how to enjoy time in the open air and the benefits it brings whether we are relaxing, bathing, eating, or working.

These days, for the many of us who are city-dwellers, open air living is a luxury. Our space is circumscribed by the four walls of our houses and the concrete expanses of the cities we live in. We feel confined, both physically and mentally, making us realize how important it is to be in touch with nature. Those lucky enough to have homes in the mountains or beside the sea or a lake, can go to the country when warm weather and vacations from work beckon. But even in the city, there is usually a park nearby, a roof terrace, balcony, or tiny patio where you can set up a folding chair and enjoy fresh air and natural light.

Cooking on the beach, eating in the backyard, sleeping under the stars, bathing in a chilly lake, and working on a shady terrace—all these things bring a feeling of expansion and freedom that puts our minds at ease and broadens our vistas.

Outdoor accoutrements for working, eating, or relaxing look good when they blend with their natural setting. Choose colors to reflect the seasons and their fruits.
above **Autumn fruits brighten up an outdoor party in a backyard.**

left **When apple season is upon you, fill baskets and sit in the fall sunshine to peel and chop the fruit.**
opposite **Raking autumn leaves is a thankless task. Stop and rest in a weathered wooden chair before you put your tools away.**

The garden is already full of flowers, but you may add your own touches of color and design. Set up a miniature tea ceremony on a city terrace, orchestrating subtle greens on a soft pink mat. Take the indoors out, and enhance nature's decor with your linens, cushions, and china. Whether you decorate using old-fashioned floral prints with delicate borders, or stark modern lines and ethnic colors, you have a whole new space in which to use your talents to create your own style and ambiance.

Big skies, green grass, and open spaces reassure us and make us happier people. A sunset on the sea's horizon, a view across a lake, the sound of a rushing river, or the broad expanse of sky seen from a city rooftop can seduce us with the promise of strength and opportunity, of peace and renewal.

It would be impossible to improve on nature's taste in design. Her celestial ceilings are higher than the dome of the grandest cathedral, her colors more vivid and profuse than in the most elegant tapestry, her textures more varied than an emporium full of fabrics, and all her elements and design are constantly moving and changing, never still, never boring.

Extending interior decoration outdoors is our way of domesticating our surroundings, making our spaces pretty and comfortable, and creating an atmosphere for entertaining or relaxing. Alfred, Lord Tennyson, recalled tea parties with a friend in London, "on those summer Sundays her drawing room was generally the garden, India rugs making patches of colour on the green, and knots of chairs and chintz-covered couches gathered under the layers of green shade of wide-spreading trees."

Gazebos, slamming screen doors, the patter of feet on decking, pools and outdoor showers, woods, streams, and beaches, all speak to us of days spent in the open air, where exercise is easy, food tastes better, life is informal.

relaxing

Whether you like the sun or shade, there is nothing more restful than spending a lazy afternoon in the backyard stretched out in a comfortable chair, on a blanket, or in a pile of pillows with a cool drink, a good book, or a couple of friends to chat with. And what could be more romantic than sleeping under the stars? Set a comfortable bed under the trees and let the sounds of nature waft you to sleep.

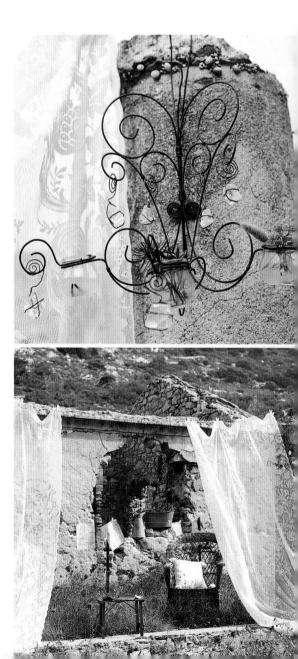

To relax you have to be comfortable, and will probably need more than just an old blanket spread on the ground to sit or lie on. Pillows help. A hammock swinging between two trees wafts you gently in the breeze. A deckchair by the pool or on the beach is fine for sunbathing. A wicker chaise longue on the lawn is a good place to read and fall asleep.

If the sun is very strong, you will need a large bottle of water to replace lost liquids and a parasol or wide-brimmed hat for shade. Or opt for a collapsible deckchair with an overhead shade made just for reading.

Even if you are stuck in the city, find a small space outdoors where you can feel the breezes. Of course, not every home has a terrace or yard. If you don't have a single spot to put a foot outdoors, simply get yourself a large burlap bag that will hold a folding chair, a pillow, and a book, and go to the nearest park to sit, read, sleep, socialize, or simply watch the ducks on the pond.

If you do have a terrace or balcony high above the city streets, start the day there, weather permitting, by reading the newspaper and drinking an early morning cup of coffee, while relaxing on a wicker sofa in front of a panoramic view. Alternatively, enjoy the last rays of the sun after a busy day's work and take your drink onto your high balcony.

On a bright morning, take a mat out onto a city rooftop and meditate on your view of the buildings and streets below you. Here is all the space you need to breathe deeply and concentrate on your mantra while you contemplate the

If you are going to do serious birdwatching and sit still for an hour or two, you must be comfortable. Take your binoculars, a bird book, and a portable chair and set it up on the edge of a marsh or a wood, where you will have an action-packed drama played out on the stage in front of you. Striped canvas is a tough and attractive fabric for outdoor pillows, and a pale-blue cotton throw brightens up the color scheme. Watch a robin building its nest, a heron on the rocks, little yellow orioles as they flutter from flower to tree, swallows chasing insects after a storm, or delicate hummingbirds as they quiver in front of the hollyhocks. Or listen to the haunting call of the coot, the gulls, and cormorants fighting over territory. Sit still, and birds will come near you, curious to know who has invaded their territory. It is also fascinating to watch the insects around you: bees, dragonflies, grasshoppers, and spiders are all part of our outdoor life.

stopping for a few moments in a quiet corner where you can commune with nature brings a sense of freedom and independence

endless sky above. You will have to concentrate hard, or use a personal stereo to block out the city noises that rise with the heat: screaming police sirens, booming fire engines, wailing ambulances, whining construction machines—and roaring planes and helicopters overhead. Or you might meditate on the noises, imagining that you are listening to a spontaneous modern symphony!

A screen porch is one of the best ways to extend your living space outdoors. Furnished and shaded by the roof, but still open to the elements and fresh air, this is a lovely place to sit all year round. Porches exist in all shapes and sizes, open to the elements, screened in or a combination of both. Wooden panels can hold floor-to-ceiling screens that keep out the bugs without destroying the impression of open air living. When summer fades, glass panels can be used to replace the screens, so this part of the porch can continue to be used for relaxing or dining all through the winter. Some porches have screens in window frames, and the glass panels are simply hinged back like shutters all summer, ready to be closed up as the seasons change.

So, whatever the season, settle into a rocking chair on the porch and keep your hands busy with knitting, needlepoint, or another relaxing and creative hobby. The porch is also a good place for a ping-pong table, a walking machine, or other exercise

opposite and above Spend a few days in a romantic retreat with the person dearest to you. Relax and reflect together while you take long walks in the surrounding woods and meadows, bicycle to a nearby town, pick flowers from the garden, and plunder the vegetable patch for your supper. Living outdoors gives you a new perspective on the daily life and problems you left behind. You don't need much indoor space—a simple one-room house gives shelter if it rains, but when the sun is shining, bring your world out into the fresh air. Use a deckchair to relax in or make a wide wooden bench comfortable with pretty printed cushions. Once gathered, fruit and vegetables are stored in baskets, and garlic hangs on the wall. A heart made of bark is a symbol of the saying, "two hearts, one beat."

left A rough wooden shelf hangs from the eaves to hold decorative plants, potted in assorted bowls and old cans.

equipment. A small table and chairs will keep children happy and give them a place to feed dolls or pets. And its large expanse of wooden floor makes the porch a safe place to race toy cars.

Arrange porch furniture in groups for talking, dining, or privacy. The furniture you choose should be light enough to move around to fit these various scenarios. For this reason, wicker is a favorite, because it is substantial enough to be comfortable, and light enough to move about easily to wherever it is needed. Also, wicker lends itself to both traditional and modern designs. You can spray paint it any color you like or leave its natural color to age to a rich brown. Canvas director's chairs also make useful and light porch furniture, and can be folded up and stored against the wall when not in use.

Match the fabrics you choose for furnishings to the setting. On a country porch, opt for faded floral linens. By the ocean you would need vivid colors

left A spacious country house in Provence makes the perfect setting for summer vacations. Big French doors beckon you outside in the morning, and a table and chairs provide a breakfast nook that catches the early morning sun.

opposite and above Extend your indoor space outdoors by bringing a bench or chaise longue into the yard and covering it with pillows from the living room. Then settle down for a midmorning cup of coffee with the newspaper. Blue and white is a favorite outdoor theme played out here with toile de jouy cotton fabric bordered in ticking and continued through to the Cornishware teacups.

above **Off to the country for the weekend. Whatever the time of year, you will need lots of baskets, wooden boxes, and strong canvas bags to use when you are there. Galoshes are essential to work in a muddy garden. In the spring you can be planting the flower and vegetable gardens. In the fall you will need to gather the harvest. There is nothing so delicious as apples picked from your own tree. Take gardening books and needlework to occupy the long summer evenings sitting out on the porch.**

because the light is stronger. Blue or green striped canvas, for instance, will slowly fade into pastel hues, while the fabric will stand up to the elements for many years. In the city, be more daring and use bold and strong colors, such as hot pink, fuchsia, or orange to enliven a background that is often gray. In winter, too, what you lack in foliage you can make up for with strong colors.

Another useful addition to a porch is the installation of electric sockets along the wall it shares with the main house. These make it easy to have lamps on tables, as well as lanterns by doors leading into the house, so you can sit outdoors long after the sun has gone down. From the comfort of your porch, you can watch the colors of the garden slowly fade in the reflected sunset, as night becomes day's negative, black and white and pearly gray.

As you sit out on your porch in the dark and listen, the sounds are magnified. Crickets chatter, frogs croak, fireflies blink, dragonflies crash into porch lights. Laughing voices and music at a distant party waft across a lake. The rigging jingles against the masts of sailboats at anchor in the bay below and waves lap against their hulls. Scents of jasmine, honeysuckle, or mock orange perfume the dark. Moonlight dances on the water and gives the trees statuesque shapes. On a moonless night, the darkness draws the world in around you.

What better way to combine relaxation with the outdoor life than to sleep out? Sleeping on a sleeping porch combines all the comforts of home with the joy of sleeping in the open. A sleeping

above and left **An armchair on the front porch provides a perfect spot to sit and watch the world go by. A quilted pillow with a contrasting border and a striped canvas cushion make the seat more comfortable. On the table is a blue spongeware mug, and a piece of homemade cake to tempt hungry children who are playing on the lawn in front of the house. As you enjoy the fresh air, occupy your hands by sewing a quilt to create an heirloom for your family. Friends passing by will stop for an informal visit and admire your handiwork.**

opposite **What could be more relaxing than settling on a grassy bank to fish, with a soft mattress and pillows to sit on, blankets to keep out the drafts, and—of course—plenty of time? Every fisherman requires patience and dedication until a likely catch takes the bait. Then there is a rush of excitement and suspense until it is landed and you see just what kind of fish you have caught—and how big it is. Clean it on the spot, light a fire, and cook a delicious picnic on the riverbank, or take it home to show off to friends and family and grill it on the barbecue for supper.**

below **For outdoor use, cover a portable mattress with tough red-and-white canvas. Hold it in place with ties at one end so it can easily be removed for cleaning. A cotton throw in a soft beige herringbone weave is useful to put over your knees.**

porch consists of a platform and roof attached to the house with floor-to-ceiling screens all the way around. Canvas shades furled up with clothesline rope are ready to be let down in case a storm comes up in the middle of the night. Otherwise, you are well placed to watch the sun rise from the sublime comfort of a warm and cozy bed.

Alternatively, you can venture a little farther from the comfort of your house and sleep under the stars on a balmy night—the epitome of romance. Avoid the dark confines of the traditional canvas tent, and take a mattress out onto the lawn or set up a cot under a swishing pine tree at the far corner of the yard. Hang a mosquito net from the branches above you to keep the bugs at bay and bring out blankets and soft pillows. Then stretch out in comfort and listen to the wind in the pines as you drift into sleep. Have an extra quilt or warm blanket to keep you warm when the coolest hour brings "the little breeze that says, 'the dawn—the dawn,' and dies away" (*The Cottage Book* by Sir Edward

rather than snooze the hours away, take the opportunity to write your journal or pick up your sketchpad

Grey). Wake up just as the sun peeks over the horizon—pure yellow to herald another perfect day.

Of course, relaxing does not only mean dreaming the hours away in slumber or collapsing into a comfortable chair with a good book. Take a trip into the world of ornithology, for example. Wherever you are, you can see or hear birds at work or play, and, if you sit quietly, they will often sally straight into your territory with all the confidence of a pet cat, hopping onto the arm of a chair or down toward your feet in search of something to eat.

Alternatively, head off on a fishing expedition. You can fish from a motorboat out at sea, or from the beach. You can wade into the middle of a rushing stream and cast with flies, or sit patiently in a rowboat or on the grassy bank and dangle your line in a lake.

Relaxation can also mean having a change of scene. You may want to head off in a painted gypsy wagon or on a hiking and camping expedition. A stream near your campsite will be essential for bathing and cooking. Your tent or wagon

A solarium makes the perfect spot for a studio. Plant a comfortable rattan chaise longue in a suitable spot and surround yourself with all the equipment you need to pursue any hobby that takes your fancy. Have books on hand for light reading, binoculars to check on an exotic bird that comes into view, a box full of paints and crayons, plus a sketchpad to record the view or a pretty face that comes your way. With pencil and paper there, make lists for next week's party or write a long-overdue letter to a friend.

relaxing **27**

may provide minimal protection from the elements, but you will have to cook, eat, wash and bathe, relax and work in the open air. Life slows down and, instead of whisking past the fields and flowers in a blur, you are able to admire them, and enjoy the scenery at your leisure. At night the campfire becomes the center of your world, and the stars, the moon, the wind, and the hooting owls will be your companions.

Escaping from roads, cars, speed, and noise is a tonic. So leave behind possessions, and crowds, responsibilities and ringing phones. If you're off on a hiking trip, check for marked paths or routes beforehand, so you do not constantly have to test the route and turn back from overhanging cliff ledges or impenetrable bush. If you are either too young or too old to carry an enormous backpack, and apt to get caught in the rain, you will probably do best to stay in motels overnight, but a welcome bath and

opposite **For a really independent vacation, why not bundle your nearest and dearest into a painted gypsy wagon and set off across England's west country or the south of France? Usually, kind farmers will let you stop in a corner of their fields, or your pony can graze on the wide verges at the side of the road. One or two bicycles can be attached to the back of the wagon to be used for exploring during the day. You will feel a real sense of freedom, not having to rely on motorized transportation.**

this page **On a beautiful fall day, pack all your grooming and riding equipment into a strong canvas bag and head down to the paddock. Bring your horse in, saddle up, and ride through the woods to enjoy the glorious colors in the countryside. The plaid horseblanket is left to warm in the sun, ready to cover your horse when it goes back to the pasture.**

games that involve the whole family and guests are a good way to work off the excesses of a weekend lunch

soft bed will do nothing to diminish your sense of independence if you hike from one destination to the next for several days in a row.

Outdoor activities are good for us all, whether it is fishing, horseriding, tennis, badminton, a game of golf, or a long walk. These are all sports that encourage us to breathe in fresh air and commune with nature—always good for our physical and mental health. Although horseriding, golf, and tennis require a certain outlay for equipment and space, jogging or walking can be done anywhere, anytime—try walking part or all of the way to work in the morning, or take an hour's walk at lunchtime to shake away the cobwebs and clear your mind. After a short time, you will become addicted to the fresh air and exercise!

Outdoor games are another way to enjoy the outdoors and take some exercise at the same time. On a smooth area of the lawn in front of your house, you might set up croquet hoops, and with a set of mallets and balls guests can have a rousing and competitive game while enjoying their predinner drinks. In England, on the village bowling green or in front of the house, young and old join

opposite and left **It is harvest time. The fruit is gathered in the orchard, and the last vegetables are pulled from the garden. On a warm Indian summer's day, a table is set up outside, decorated with colorful corn cobs, pumpkins and squash. This perambulating table has a wheel on the front and handles behind so it can be moved into the sun, out of the wind, wherever you want to have your party. Serve freshly made cider from a stoneware pitcher. Glasses in straw holders complete the autumnal scene.**
below **Children love to raid the costume box to dress up a scarecrow and surround him with pumpkins.**

opposite The owner of this red clapboard house has built a rustic arbor in his garden. With slender tree trunks, which he cut in the surrounding woods, he made a simple frame in Adirondack style. No attempt is made to hide the knots and bark on the unfinished wood. Eventually the frame will support climbing plants and hanging baskets.

this page A little white porch makes an extension of a children's playhouse—an inviting place to set the stage for imaginative play. The children's world is populated by dolls, a wooden horse, and old-fashioned games that have been collected and kept in good repair for generation after generation. Ragdolls sit on the Shaker-style red bench (see page 130), and autumn leaves brighten up a spongeware pitcher. A piece of an old paisley shawl and a remnant of a pretty quilt have been used to make lovely pillows. Birds can watch the activity from their houses hung high on the porch beams.

in a game of lawn bowls, carefully rolling heavy balls across the grass toward a smaller ball. The winner is the one who gets his balls closest to the first ball. Variations of this game are played in many countries: the Italians have *bocce*, the South Slavs play *balinaje*, and, of course, *boules* is famously played in villages throughout France. Garden quoits is another gentle garden game; it needs four rope quoits and a wooden stand with five scoring pegs.

Playing in the open air brings out the child in all of us. In fact, the nineteenth-century Romantics believed that we should respond to nature the way a child does—instinctively, simply, joyfully. Childhood experiences of nature may form our emotional and mental responses to life as adults. Creative children can turn any everyday place or object into a wonderland. Rocks become the rooms of a house or palace. Sandcastles become bastions of last surrender in front of the attack of the incoming tide. Rivers and streams, sticks and stones, bushes and trees all become hideouts in a world of fairies and princesses, pirates and cowboys. A terrace, out of sight of the grownups, may provide a stage for young singers and dancers. And a band of cousins dress up in costumes and then make up a play around their newly acquired personae.

Tepees make excellent hideaways and a homemade version can easily be constructed. The whole family will be

below **This metal and wood sofa has elegant touches of neoclassical style. Its built-in shelf holds candles to set the mood when the sun goes down. The seat is covered with an old French quilt, and another makes a comfortable throw in the evening.**

opposite **This half-indoor, half-outdoor studio is adapted from an old barn. One side of the building is completely open to the elements, making it easy to move large works of art and furniture to waiting transportation outside. The artist who works here builds iron furniture and decorates extraordinary pieces of wood. His special world is screened from everyday life by huge theatrical curtains, which he has painted with poetic landscapes.**

This exotic roof-top terrace exhibits a striking mix of unusually strong colors. A deep purple mattress lies on the floor with striped bolsters, and large cotton sheets in red, white, and blue are hung overhead for shade. Melon looks appetizing on a hammered Turkish tray, and eggplant-colored glasses on a wire tray cast a patchwork of shadows across the old tiled floor. Here, the owner of the house reads, listens to music, and contemplates the view of the countryside covered in vineyards, sloping down to the pale sea beyond.

needed to help set it up in the backyard or in a clearing in the woods. Ten wooden poles are firmly embedded in the ground at an angle so they all meet in a central spot and can be tied together about three quarters of the way up. Cover them with waterproof canvas, leaving a opening on one side. Let light in through the opening or under a short hem around the bottom. It is not a bad idea to put canvas on the ground inside so that any blankets and pillows borrowed from the house won't be sitting on damp grass. And make sure there is a hitching post outside where residents and visitors can tether real or imaginary ponies. Birds' feathers collected in the surrounding area are useful for making headdresses, writing pens, decoration, or to trade. A good supply of beads and some plastic wire will be useful for making jewelry and wampum. Messages can be written on pieces of birchbark and sent to neighboring tribes, who might be perched in a nearby treehouse.

Treehouses are another exotic place to disappear to, where you can pull up the ladder and escape life's humdrum existence. A plywood platform, however small, makes a good floor, and

below and right **Don't feel guilty if, from time to time, you feel the need to take time out from the daily rush to be alone. Peace and solitude are essential for everyone, but they can seem impossible to find in a crowded and noisy city. Why not disappear to a secluded corner high on the roof for a few hours? You need only a few items with you: a mat to lie on, a small pillow, a tea set for a herbal tea, and a book to help you meditate.**

sides can be constructed with wood, canvas, or just old blankets hung on the surrounding branches. You can build a nest inside— a really comfortable place for reading, storytelling, or exchanging secrets with your best friend.

Grownups, too, have a history of escaping into the trees. The Roman Emperor Caligula held banquets in the branches of an enormous plane tree. In Renaissance Italy the Medicis built a palace in the sky complete with plumbing, marble benches, a fountain, and two staircases. Historic examples of elaborate treehouses still survive in Europe, such as the sixteenth-century treehouse at Pitchford Hall, England, and the tree-church in Allouville-Bellefosse, Normandy.

Willow houses are another natural play place that bring life to a backyard or nearby field. Willow branches are stuck into the ground and then bent to shape an arbor seat, or a tunnel in the shape of a dragon, or even a little house. The thicker branches make the outline, and thinner ones are woven through, horizontally and laterally. With bendy live willow branches you can make doors and windows wherever you want them in a tepee or house. Eventually leaves will sprout over the whole structure, and can be closely clipped to make its leafy green covering. And, of course, as the willows grow, the whole structure gets bigger—the sky's the limit!

And we must not forget the sturdy old-fashioned playhouse with shiplap boarding, windows with stationary shutters, an opening door, solid wooden roof, and flooring. Tucked away in the far corner of the backyard, this will be the scene of a myriad imaginative happenings for several generations.

find a small space outdoors where you can feel the breezes and meditate on a distant view

above and left **Even if you live in cooler climes, you can still give your surroundings an exotic, Eastern flavor by planting palms and bamboo in sunny corners of the backyard. Palm trees in brown Chinese pots convey a feeling of hospitality and easy living. With a trolley on rollers they** **can be moved to a sheltered spot in the winter. String up a pole hung with Chinese lanterns in front of the bamboo, lie back, and listen to them rustling and whispering together in the warm breeze. When darkness closes in, carefully light them to create an oriental party mood.**

bathing

Bathing in fresh water or salt water is always good for your body and your peace of mind. An early morning swim sets you up for the day ahead. A plunge in the swimming pool cools you off in the heat of the noonday sun. A long walk on the beach and a swim in the ocean gives you all the exercise you need. Wash off the salt and sand under an outdoor shower and dry off in a thick cotton robe.

You don't need much equipment for the ultimate in shoreside luxury. Set up a white awning on the wet sand right by the water's edge as the tide goes out. An old folding cot makes a perfect place to read, rest, and relax. Take a canvas mattress and matching pillow for added comfort, and a little folding table. Set up camp and then stride off for a long walk down the beach.

Very early in the morning, leap out of bed, fling on a robe, and head to the swimming rocks for a skinny dip. As the sun comes up from behind the village on the distant shore, it tells the weather report for the day: pale yellow promises perfect sunshine; rosy pink is deceptively beautiful—"red sky at morning, sailors take warning."

The rest of the world sleeps, and the glassy water barely moves, waiting for the morning breeze to come. Just one early motorboat breaks the silence a mile away, speeding up to fresh fishing grounds at the head of the lake. The gulls and ducks have already had their breakfast, and pretend to be asleep, but they keep a keen eye out for danger. At the approach of a swimmer, mother duck decides not to take any chances and leads her brood away from the rocks, quacking at them all to keep in line and stay behind her. The gulls are more daring, and balance tenuously on their rocks, nervously shaking their feathers as they eye the intruder.

The cold water is invigorating; the breaststroke replaces routine limbering-up exercises. Shampoo your hair, then dive in again to rinse. The clear, soft water will make your hair shine more than it ever did in the shower at home. What a treat to arrive at the breakfast table feeling hungry, energized, and ready for whatever the day ahead may bring.

heaven is diving into the surf, walking miles up and down the beach looking for shells, feeling the hot sun on your back, falling asleep under a palm tree

The beach, it has to be said, is a lovely place to get bronzed, hot, sandy, and salty—but not clean. The salt lightens your hair, makes your nails hard, and the sand is a natural way to exfoliate your skin. One way to stay clean and comfortable at the beach is to take a folding cot to lie on. Put up four poles and attach a tent made from chiffon or voile to keep off the wind and the flies. Alternatively, carry a folding chair and a pure white umbrella down to just above the water's edge, and settle here to read or watch the view while your generous umbrella keeps you cool and protected from the sun.

After a day at the beach, you will be feeling hot and sandy—and the best thing in the world is stepping under an outdoor shower. The clear water is so refreshing as it washes off the salt and sand from head to toe. Take a rest, put on fresh cotton clothes, and start the evening feeling healthy from a day in the sunshine.

If the beach is too far, or you prefer to avoid the sand, a few hours of lazing by the pool are the answer. Awaiting you at the swimming pool are comfortable deckchairs, a shady parasol, and tables on which to put your book, glass, telephone. Relax to your heart's content, and when you are too hot, it's only two steps to a refreshing swim.

When you have walked for miles up to the end of the beach and back, collapse on a cot and hide from the sun's strong rays under a lightweight tent. Construct your tent (see page 120) from bright red, orange, and blue voile or organza—you might not think of them as outdoor fabrics, but they are soft and billowing, and come in an array of bright colors that look striking beside the ocean. Use them to surround your cot, and feel as if you are resting in an oriental bazaar on the beach. The cover will keep out the bugs, filter the sun, and act as a windbreak. To make a comfortable mattress, sew an envelope from a striped straw rug, fill it with a layer of foam, and leave the frayed ends to overhang your bed. A cotton throw keeps you warm if the air cools in the late afternoon. When the sun goes down, just fold up your room and take it home in a big straw basket.

This is the life! On a hot summer afternoon, pack a bag and take your book, glasses, and drink out to the pool. Relax under the oleanders on a makeshift bed with a pile of downy pillows made from brightly colored silk at your back. When it gets too hot, sit on the stone steps of the pool and let the water cool your legs and feet while you continue to read or chat with friends. Later on, plunge into the cooling waters. An outdoor faucet makes a fitting water inlet for the stone pool. Rounded urns soften the angular dimensions of the pool's shape and could be planted with decorative geraniums and oleanders.

tray full of watermelon, cookies, lemonade, and water for everyone to help themselves. Even if you don't bathe, the poolside is a comfortable area for conversation and reading, because your deckchair and mattress are there.

The pool should be surrounded by paving stones or decking; grass is not ideal because the dirt gets into the water. Use your gardening skills around its borders—the curves of large pots at either end can soften the straight lines of a rectangular pool. Sit in the sun and the shade—climbing roses on an arbor are decorative and provide a shady place to sit or eat.

A pool house is a convenient place to store equipment and provides a useful changing room for wet swimmers. Architecturally, it should harmonize with the main house, but a less substantial shelter can easily be camouflaged by a trellis full of honeysuckle and clematis. A paved piazza in front of the pool house is a level spot for a barbecue and dining table. Shade it with a big white canvas umbrella.

A wall near the pool will provide shelter from the wind and, when covered with huge colorful cushions, converts to a comfy sofa for poolside parties. Encourage the children to look for special rocks, birds' eggs, pinecones, shells,

Pools range from oversized bathtubs where you can loll, to vast stretches of water where you are challenged to do enough lengths to qualify for your daily exercise. Invite friends to come for lunch and spend the afternoon. You can lie on floats and chat in the pool while the children entertain themselves jumping in and out of the water. Cover a nearby table with a bright cloth, and bring out a

A poolhouse is both decorative and useful.
Normally it should reflect the architectural style
of the main house. Plants climbing an arbor on the
front provide shade, as does a big white umbrella
on the paved area around to the pool. Swimmers
can change here without dripping water all through
the house, and there is room to store deckchairs,
umbrellas, and pool toys out of season. Stowed
away on shelves inside are big pool towels and
soap to use in the outdoor shower at the back. In
the privacy of a grove of bamboo trees, this is a
good place to rinse off and wash your hair. In the
evening, turn on the underwater lights and arrange
lanterns around the pool. It makes a perfect setting
for drinks at dusk or after-dinner conversation in
the dark—or even a midnight swim.

and any other treasures that take their fancy. They can display their collections on top of the wall.

If you are constricted by city spaces, what a treat to have a Jacuzzi on your roof terrace! Sit in the hot tub with your head in the fresh air even on a cold winter's night to clear your thoughts and stimulate your circulation. In peace and privacy far above the urban bustle, make a green oasis around the tub. Do fresh-air exercises when you get out of the hot water—it should be just as effective as taking a sauna and rolling in the snow, and will undo all the bad effects of central heating. When not in use, cover the jacuzzi to keep out city grime and wandering wildlife.

Outdoor swimming can take its toll on your hair, as you are constantly having to wash away the sand and salt from the beach or chemicals from the swimming pool. The answer is to give your hair a natural deep-conditioning treatment by massaging oils through the dry ends before washing. Even some warm olive oil left to work on your hair for half an hour will make all the difference. The herbs in your garden also contain wonderful oils that can benefit your hair while their aroma soothes the mind. Try rinsing your hair with an infusion of lavender, rosemary, thyme, or sage leaves, or chamomile flowers for fair hair. Or, a traditional and very natural way to clean your hair is using an egg!

bathing in cool clear rivers will invigorate your skin, leaving it glowing with good health

Nature is a rich source of beauty treatments, and many concoctions have been created over the centuries claiming to have miraculous results. A seventeenth-century French collection describes a sachet powder used by Queen Isabella of Spain, combining rose leaves, orris root, calamus, storax, benzoin, giroffe flowers, and coriander. There are plenty of simpler natural beauty treatments you can make yourself, using the herbs and fruits of your garden, essential oils, and the contents of your pantry. Before trying any natural beauty treatment, however, always do a patch test and leave it overnight to check that you are not allergic to any of the ingredients.

To refresh tired-looking skin, mix a handful of sea salt with oil to make an effective body scrub. Or, add sea salt to your bathwater, lie back, and enjoy its natural benefits. Milk, too, will leave your skin feeling smooth and soft, so add a few cupfuls to the water to indulge in a Cleopatra-style bath. Or, turn to the garden again and gather a bundle of

left and above left **Bathe in a cool rushing stream, and feel at one with the elements. Only a few props are needed—nature provides the rest.**
right **Where the river bends, there is a tiny island where the water is crystal clear. Spend a morning here bathing, washing your hair, and indulging in natural body care. When you are clean and refreshed, slip on a crisp white dress—and feel wonderful!**
far right **Even shaving outdoors has its advantages: no hurry, birds singing, and fresh air smelling of lavender. All you need is a folding mirror, a basin for soap, a razor, shaving brush and cream, and a towel.**

lavender, rosemary, or rose petals. Wrap them in a cheesecloth bag to hang under the hot running water of your bath for a relaxing and fragrant soak.

Other natural beauty products that may be on offer in your garden or pantry are avocados, pineapples, and cucumbers. All these are wonderful for your skin and can be puréed and applied as face masks, or simply pop a couple of cucumber slices over your eyes and take the opportunity to contemplate the day in a shady corner of the backyard.

The best natural tonics for beautiful skin and hair are, of course, fresh air, exercise, nutritious food, and plenty of sleep and relaxation—the recipe for a healthy and happy life.

eating

Eating outdoors adds another dimension of festivity and wellbeing to one's taste and enjoyment of food. Outdoor parties have a gala air that is difficult to duplicate inside. Children love the freedom to run around, and then eat on their knees, or seated on the ground. Even the most humble picnic carried to the beach or snacks eaten out on the lawn taste all the better for the open skies overhead.

At the end of this garden, the gazebo makes a focal point, standing out among the flowers and bushes. On the first warm spring day, set up a table here and invite the whole family to join you outdoors. The blues and patterns of the tablecloth (see page 128) pick up the flowers and colors in the garden. The china is decorated with a similar pattern of leaves, and the teacups and teapot reiterate the floral theme. Serve Lapsang Souchong or Earl Grey tea, plus cool lemonade for the children with plenty of muffins, preserves, cookies, and little cakes for hungry visitors who may drop by. They will want to come back again and again during the summer months.

Eating in the open air should be enjoyed all year round. Vary your meals and snacks with the changing seasons. On the first sunny afternoons, arrange a romantic tea under the rose arbor. Set the table with a floral tablecloth and delicate painted china. On a large tray, bring out a pot of Lapsang Souchong and a Gateau Basque, a delicious buttery cake filled with black cherry preserves. Concentrate on the changing colors of the sky and the mountains, a Verdi aria drifting out from the radio into the open air, the running water in the river, the calm sunset.

On a hot weekend you may choose to lay two Moroccan carpets and enormous pillows in a corner of the backyard under the bamboo grove and serve brunch while you listen to the sound of Japanese bells hanging in the bamboo. Or prepare a huge bowl of fruit salad with the first strawberries of the season, and serve them on the lawn or by the swimming pool with iced tea flavored with mint leaves. And, when the sun is scorching hot, shelter under a shady tree or trellis with a bright checked cloth and wicker hamper spread out on the cool grass. Or, in a sheltered courtyard, a bowl piled high with tropical fruits and pitchers of freshly squeezed limeade are always appreciated by hot and hungry visitors.

In the fall, turn to orange and red colors for cloths that harmonize with the foliage above your table. This is a good time to use a mobile barbecue and grill hamburgers and hotdogs when there is a chill in the air. In the winter months most outdoor eating is done standing up—drinking hot soup from a thermos while watching a game of football or a skating competition, or treat yourself to a rum toddy in the back of a sleigh.

opposite **If you keep a weather-resistant metal table and chairs in a corner of the yard, they are easily transformed into a pretty table when the sun is shining and it is nicer to be outdoors than in. Bring out tea and cake on a tray and invite a friend to join you in a tête-à-tête. Luxuriate in the space around you, giving a feeling of privacy that will encourage** confidences from your guest. **Creamy white Wedgwood china is refined and elegant, and an old-fashioned flowered tablecloth gives a special touch to your afternoon tea. Its pretty printed pattern sports a solid-colored border that reflects the tones of the china and makes it hang beautifully on this round table.**

this page **Surround yourself with flowers: on your china, on your tablecloth, and on the ground all around you.**

The tradition of cooking and eating outdoors is as old as fire. And, although our modern tastes have developed with the introduction of international foods to our diets, our methods of cooking in the open air have barely changed over the last ten thousand years.

We still start with a fire and then cook our foods on a rack or spit, or smoke or roast them in an ovenlike pit—just as the cavemen did.

"Barbe à queue!" the Frenchman exclaimed when he saw Native Americans roasting a whole pig in an open pit. A more likely root of the name given to this style of cooking is from the Spanish term, "*barbacoa*," for the Haitian method of cooking meat on a frame over the fire. Whatever the true origin of the name, what is certain is that these days, modern gourmets know that any kind of meat, fish, or vegetable tastes better cooked over an open fire and eaten in the open air.

Clambakes and luaus are popular open air cooking methods in the United States. They are traditionally held on the beach, where it is easy to dig a hole in the sand. The hole is lined with rocks, and a fire is built in the bottom and allowed to burn down to hot coals.

For a clambake, collect the clams near the water's edge while the fire is burning down and clean them with a sharp knife. Then spread a thick layer of seaweed or leaves on the hot

When friends are coming over to spend the day, to swim and eat outdoors with you, get everything ready beforehand. Cantaloupe makes a refreshing snack for the children who are running everywhere, exploring and playing. Lemonade and fruit juice mixed with sparkling water are thirst-quenching, too. Keep the flies away with a cotton net and wire cover, which is light enough to reveal the tempting goodies underneath and still protect them. It is best to use sturdy glasses and plates outside on a stone table and floor. Unbreakable clear plastic glasses are also useful when a lot of children are around.

on long hot days, when children and adults spend all hours outdoors, a spread of cool fruit and juice will disappear quickly

plan picnics
several days in
advance so,
when the great
day arrives,
children will
be filled with
anticipation

opposite **Gather flowers and foliage
from nearby to decorate the "table,"
and serve freshly picked fruit in
baskets. Plaid blankets spread on the
ground will keep out any chills.**

this page **In the summers of childhood it never
seems to rain. Life outdoors allows the young the
freedom to be imaginative and enjoy life to the
full. Picnics in the countryside are a real treat
—no need to sit up straight at the table with a
knife and fork. Eating al fresco means having
your pick from a spread of radishes, sandwiches
made from fresh French bread, cheese and**
crackers, slices of salami, and piles of fresh
fruit. Pack all these delicacies in wicker
baskets, along with spring water, a bottle of
lemonade for the children and wine for the
grown-ups, a thermos of coffee, knives and forks,
plates, a bright checked tablecloth, and pillows
to sit on. And, once you have eaten your fill, take
turns telling stories until it is time to go home.

ashes, and put into this makeshift oven clams, lobsters, fish, potatoes, and corn on the cob in the husks. Cover with more seaweed and arrange a piece of canvas on top. Weigh the canvas down with several large rocks and steam for up to two hours. Then dig in to the most delicious meal of your life.

The luau is a very similar method of cooking to the clam bake. It is a closed-pit oven imported from the Polynesian Islands to Hawaii and then adapted by mainland Americans to suit smaller occasions, but it is still the most exotic, and perhaps the easiest, way to feed a large crowd. It involves digging and lining a pit big enough for the fish (try a whole sea bass) or whole pig that you want to roast. You then cover them with banana leaves and leave to cook for at least five hours.

Whether you are planning a clambake or luau at the beach, a riverside barbecue, or simply a spread of cold foods in the park, picnics are always fun—and children love them. On the morning of the picnic, everyone helps to fill baskets with knives and forks, cups and glasses, plates and napkins, a bag for trash and a tablecloth to put on the ground. And for the cook, pack butter and oil, paper and matches to start the fire, grills and a huge skillet, a coffeepot, and a long-handled fork and spatula. And don't forget the corkscrew! Bring a stool for the cook, and folding chairs for grandparents—everyone else can sit on the ground.

In the kitchen, preparations include parboiling the potatoes, preparing the salad, making the dressing in a jar with a tight lid, and baking the brownies.

Eventually the picnickers set out in one large boat, or even two, to find a favorite spot on the river shore that has flat rocks where the boats can land. After unloading and setting up for supper, the young are delegated to find firewood before they can run off to fish and swim. Each newly caught fish is proudly presented to the assembled company, usually still hooked to the line that waves from the rod, until a grownup offers to unhook and clean it to prepare it for grilling.

As the sun falls toward the western horizon, it is time to start the cocktail hour and begin to cook. A traditional shore dinner never changes. Bacon is fried in the big skillet, and bread toasted in the grills to make an irresistible hors d'oeuvre. "Picnic potatoes" brown in the bacon fat while the fish and hamburgers are cooking on the grills held over the fire by willing volunteers. The corn on the cob boils in a large pot full of water. What a feast—naturally any fisherman can eat his catch, and hopefully there are some extra perch for the rest of

this page **These sturdy stools are ideal outdoor furnishings and are easy to make at home (see page 136). Knots and rough bark are proudly displayed in true Adirondack style!**
opposite **When the hay has been gathered in and the trees are heavy with fruit, prepare an impromptu picnic with the simplest but most delicious food. Pack cheese, cold meat, bread, and beer in a basket, and transport it with stools and a portable table to a secluded spot, gathering fresh fruit as you walk. Leave the stools to weather in your secret picnic place, and they will be there when you return to eat, paint, or rest on your walk.**

On a hot summer's day, invite friends on the spur of the moment to spend an afternoon at your pool. When they feel hot and thirsty, nothing is better than fresh watermelon served on a deck table. The big white umbrella provides welcome shade. China and glasses in cool green and aqua colors take up the theme of the water and fruit. Even the spoons have blue handles. Your guests will appreciate this refreshing treat as well as your talent for making a stunning still-life with natural colors.

the family to enjoy, too. There is a lull in the conversation while appetites are satisfied, then traditional subjects of conversation are piqued—stories of the olden days, memories of mischief-making, then turning to jokes and ghost stories as the night darkens, all part of the traditional atmosphere, recreated by each generation for the next.

Finally it is time to pack up and go home—hopefully, someone will have remembered to bring a flashlight! It is crucial to make

sure no sign of the picnic remains: put out the fire with water from the cooking pot, and make a line to pass the gear to a packer in the boat. Finally, all jump aboard and push off—home again after another wonderful picnic.

If you are traveling on foot rather than by boat, it can be quite a burden to carry your picnic with you. The answer, of course, is to arrange for it to be set up ahead of you. The most agreeable hiking vacations are those organized by an agency that sends the luggage ahead from one hotel to the next and sets up the day's lunch for you at a halfway spot. A friend recounted an elegant picnic she had while hiking in Spain. As she says, this menu would be exotic in any setting: "Ideally, you also need the

A sophisticated dinner party is set up on the beach at St. Tropez. Everything is carried down along a long pathway cut through the bamboo grove. The beach pavilion makes a perfect setting for outdoor dining, with a deck floor to provide a level surface for the table and chairs, and poles supporting a wood-tiled roof for shelter. Guests dress up after sundown and waft along the path of decking lined with tiny candles that give a romantic glow. Nature enhances the lighting and sound, with the full moon sparkling on the sea, and the soothing sounds of waves swishing in and out on the beach.

shade of some spreading cork trees, a hot and cloudless sky, and a long, dreamy view across the Andalusian sierras. But it will taste almost as good on a chilly patch of a mountain park."

This Mediterranean picnic started with tapas of fresh anchovy filets marinated in oil and garlic, salted almonds, little squares of manchego cheese and quince jelly served with walnuts, and spiced pears with breaded veal cutlets. Guests were also offered stuffed eggs and slices of pata negra ham, chorizo, olives, raisins swollen with powerful Spanish brandy, fritters made with tiny crevettes, beans stewed for hours with pieces of ham, and tomato salad with slivers of sweet onion. This was followed by white gazpacho made with blanched almonds, garlic, day-old bread, olive oil vinegar, salt, and water—all whizzed into soup in a food processor. The main course and *pièce de résistance* was cold grilled quails, which had stood overnight in a lemon juice marinade before being broiled next morning under a high heat for about seven minutes, breasts down to absorb the juice, and turned over for a minute or two to brown. The quails were accompanied by a Spanish tortilla—a thick potato omelet made with eggs, potatoes, artichokes, sausage, onion, olive oil, and salt. All was happily washed down with quantities of icy cold Spanish rosé.

below and below right **The table is set for a sparkling evening. White lilies in a large glass jar set the sophisticated tone for the party. The tablecloth carries a tiny flower print in neutral colors, with an elegant organdy border. Plates, bowls, and the handles on the flatware are made from thick iced glass to complement the heavy fluted pitcher and wine glasses and to complete the soft color scheme.**

be brave with your use of color and design in an outdoor dining area. Splash colors together, mix patterns, use painted pottery plates and bowls

varieties, and coffee is served from a flask in little porcelain cups before the whole family retires for a siesta under one beach umbrella!

More and more often these days, summer concerts, operas, and theater performances are held in the open air, and the spectators take picnics to eat in the interval. These tend to be formal occasions, where the guests are dressed in their finest clothes. Folding tables and chairs are set up and laid with a damask tablecloth, silver, flowers, and candles under glass. Naturally the picnic has been made ahead of time, and standards are high. Courses are presented one by one, before the entertainment starts in the late afternoon sun, during a long intermission as twilight sets in, and at the end of the evening by the light of the moon, helped with candles under hurricane lamps.

As guests arrive and find their hostess' table set up, they are offered a welcoming drink and appetizers that

opposite **Outdoors is the place to use bold ethnic patterns on cloths and cushions. Pick an earthy scheme of orange, yellow, and green, and collect handmade pottery and African kikoyes in unusual designs. Mix and match materials to enliven a table and chairs made from old planks, and shield off the dining area with straw blinds.**
above **On a bright African kikoye, a pineapple and bowls look as glamorous as a Gaugin painting.**

A more modest, French-style picnic at the beach could include melon and prawns, French bread filled with tomatoes and cheese or salami, paté, egg dishes, aspic, and gelatin. Dessert usually consists of little pots of yogurt of different

constitute the first course. This might be quails' eggs with celery salt, raw vegetables with a tasty dip, or stuffed mushrooms. Between acts, a summer dinner might include poached salmon with a delicious green herb sauce, new potatoes, and salad. There is time to linger afterward over strawberries and cream, followed by homemade chocolates with coffee from a thermos.

"Tailgate" picnics are far more casual affairs, at sports events where vehicles are lined up side by side in the parking lot, with lots of room behind for setting up tables and chairs, or standing around while the tailgate serves as a buffet table. Normally the food has been made at home; cooking is not part of the tradition. There should always be enough extra drink and finger food for friends who make the rounds and suddenly pop up from between the cars for a chat. Raw vegetables with a curry mayonnaise dip are good handouts with a glass of wine. A main course of chicken and rice paella with crisp green salad, blue cheese, and French bread will keep healthy appetites at bay. In a tight space, disposable plastic plates— the ones that sit in wicker holders—cups and flatware are easiest to deal with. They can all be put into a big black plastic bag and thrown away when you get home. The wicker plate holders are clean and ready for the next picnic.

The setting is simple. The food is fresh. If you prefer a more restrained, uncluttered look for your courtyard dining, use the natural palette of fruit to provide a color scheme against wood and leaf-green pottery. The surrounding trees and plants will complement them. A wrought-iron chandelier, hanging from a branch of the tree that shades the table, will add a romantic glow of warm-colored lights after dark.

Of course, eating outside is not restricted to picnics and outings. Entertaining a crowd is never easy, but can be far less stressful if you utilize your lawn or patio instead of trying to squeeze everyone inside the house. Outdoor dining is less formal and restricted; guests can dress more casually, and the party can spread out a bit, particularly if your backyard is big enough for games like croquet or bowls.

For a large crowd, put tables on the lawn, not far from the barbecue, on which to serve the food and drink. If you don't have a permanent, built-in grill, an oil barrel cut in half and covered with several grills makes a good and substantial alternative. Start burning the charcoal early in the day, and the hot embers will add a special flavor to all your chicken legs and hamburgers, spareribs and sausages, vegetable kebabs, and ears of corn.

indulge the bolder side of your decorative urges and have fun looking for bits and pieces that will enliven your outdoor table

An Asian-themed picnic makes a change in accessories as well as menu. Carry food and drink in a silk bag and large tea caddy. Sushi looks delicious on pretty Chinese enamel plates, and a paper parasol will keep the sun's rays off your wooden slat table. Mix pillows in lavender, purple, and hot pink to bring your picnic spot alive with color and texture.

with appropriate colors and special props, a city patio may be transformed to celebrate any season or occasion

You can bake potatoes right in the coals at one end of the grill and serve them with plenty of butter and sour cream. A couple of large salads and lots of French bread will round off a hearty lunch. Provide plenty of iced tea, fresh lemonade, beer, and wine, and your guests will be guaranteed to have a lovely day—as long as you add a "weather permitting" note to your invitations!

A favorite meal on the farm for serving at outdoor parties is crispy Peking duck. Start by hanging a plucked and cleaned duck on the branch of a tree so it becomes "air-dried" as it waves in the wind. During the day make thin pancakes and prepare the scallions and the Chinese black sauce, which you will need that evening. At dinner time, oil the duck and cook it on a rotisserie over a blazing grill. The result: ultra-crisp skin, and the meat inside will be moist and succulent. With all the trimmings this will be a memorable Peking duck.

A teenage party is an all-day affair, and the key words with hungry, restless teenagers are quantity and variety. Young people need lots to eat and plenty to do, so provide them with such entertainment as volleyball, football, croquet, tennis, a treasure hunt, or a scavenger hunt. And let them do a good share of the cooking—kids like to show their skill with skillet and tongs. In

With imagination and ingenuity, a small city yard is transformed for an autumnal cocktail party. Linen and pillows in orange, red, and gold colors set the theme. Golden plates, decorative pumpkins and corn, **chopsticks in raffia holders, and Chinese lanterns hanging from the branches are festive accessories. Even the food blends into the color scheme.**

addition to the basic menu of hamburgers and hotdogs, try to have as many assorted relishes, spreads, quick drink mixes, and cold cuts as possible. Rolls should be of different sizes and shapes—and include some loaves of French bread for the hero-sandwich fanciers. Put out some pizza mix and toppings for those who like to make their own. Ice cream, cakes, and popcorn are wonderful extra treats.

For these backyard parties, standard equipment includes a barbecue of one variety or another—a kettle on wheels, with a shelf below for bottle storage and two side shelves for the preparation of food, or a two-tiered metal grate that allows for cooking at different temperatures. There are also tandoor ovens that heat up to very high temperatures in order to cook succulent tikka and tandoori dishes inside the hood. Variations of the Japanese *hibachi*, an insulated pail with a grill on top, are decorative as well as useful on a patio or terrace.

left **There is no need for you to leave town in order to enjoy the delights of warm summer days. Take some time off work and stay at home, where you can enjoy being outdoors on your own roof terrace. Blue and white is a fresh-looking, clean color combination for a picnic on a city terrace and is reminiscent of summer days spent at the beach. Set up in a sunny corner with a portable barbecue and a long table to hold food and equipment. The blue-and-white theme runs through all the accessories here: table mats, dishtowels, plates, and bowls. Even the olive oil is served from a Delft pitcher and the water pitcher and glasses on a woven straw tray have blue rims.**
opposite and below **Bamboo handles on the flatware and plain wooden handles on the barbecue utensils look fresh against the blue-and-white color scheme and the background of plants and red tiles.**

In addition to the barbecue, you will need a sturdy table or large cutting surface, tongs for turning grilled foods and for plucking potatoes and corn from the fire, a sprinkler bottle for controlling the flame, pliers to tighten the holding forks on the spit and to position it, skewers, and utensils from the kitchen such as drip pans, spoons, forks, and knives, a basting brush, heatproof gloves, and a meat thermometer.

Cooking equipment for campers or beach picnickers needs to be portable, and thus simpler than the barbecues you use in your backyard. A small stainless steel barrel barbecue is a sleek, Italian-styled cooker, light enough to carry to the woods or the beach. Use it either as a compact cylinder with one grill and a windbreak or folded out flat for a generous double grill area. A Scotch grill is the modern version of a *hibachi*, an insulated pail with a grill top and cover that can be filled with briquets—or food—and carried to the picnic site. Campers can put a chicken or roast into a Dutch oven. Seal it with flour and water paste, then, while they are out on the trail, it is left to cook for several hours in a pit covered with hot ashes and earth. To consolidate packing, you may just want to take a grilling rack, or a basket grill with long handles. Both of these light implements will hold food and rest on rocks while you cook over a fire built from wood you have gathered from around your picnic site.

Closer to home it is not necessary to cook outdoors in order to enjoy eating in the open air. On a summer evening, invite guests into the

opposite **On a warm summer evening, have a traditional barbecue on a city rooftop. Tonight the color scheme is red, white, and blue. Hamburgers in buns, crisp salads, and ice-cold drinks are easy to prepare, and it all tastes better for being cooked and eaten outside.**
top **Barbecue utensils are conveniently kept in a canvas holder, so they can be easily stored in the kitchen later.**
above **A steel trolley on wheels brings all your ingredients from the kitchen to the terrace. Woven metal bowls and baskets hold freshly rinsed organic fruits and vegetables.**

backyard to have a drink and watch the sun go down. Bring the table and chairs out from the dining room and set them up on the terrace or level area next to the house. Lay the table with your best linen, china, and silver, and put glass hurricane lamps over the candles. String twinkling lights in the trees overhead to create a fairyland setting.

Dinner should be in keeping with the setting. Begin with small cups of hot, double-strength consommé with chopped parsley and melba toast. The main course might be chicken "chaud-froid"— poached chicken breasts covered in a velouté sauce, decorated with truffle slices and tarragon leaves, and then set in aspic. Even though it may be complicated to prepare, this elegant dish will be a winner with your guests. And for your peace of mind, it will be made and ready to serve long before the guests arrive. A large avocado, lambs' lettuce, and nasturtium salad will go well with the chicken. To refresh the palette, try frozen

right Buy freshly caught sardines from a fisherman who is just unloading his catch on the beach, and cook them in a little hibachi pot with a grill rack on top. This is easy to carry down to the beach, and you can add bits of driftwood to its coals.
above right **Send your companions for a long walk on the beach to breathe in the ocean air and build up healthy appetites before reassembling for a picnic** on the dunes. It is a good idea to lay your tablecloth in the lee of a windbreaker, which protects you—and your spread—from the wind and sand, but still lets you enjoy the view. A cushion on a wooden crate makes a comfortable place to perch above the sand, from where you can serve your guests with fish straight from the grill, juicy tomatoes, fresh bread, and plenty of spring water and wine.

raspberry mousse for dessert with homemade *feuilles de palmier* cookies. Coffee, chocolates, and conversation will keep your guests entranced until the candles burn low and the sky begins to glow with the pale light of dawn.

An outdoor wedding is a magical event in the countryside and offers another occasion to create a really special and festive atmosphere outside. Nostalgia for old-fashioned tradition is piqued by the sight of fields full of wildflowers, girls with garlands in their hair, long dresses billowing in the breeze as the wedding party returns from the church down a country lane. The first stop is in a field beside the lane that leads to the house. Here, a table is set up to welcome guests with a cool drink and

On a baking hot summer's day, transfer your picnic from land to sea. On board, the soft, cooling breeze takes the heat off the day as you sail slowly up the coast. You won't want to cook, so prepare the food before you leave in the morning. Pasta salad, fresh tomatoes and olives, sliced ham and salami, a large camembert cheese and bread will make a delicious lunch, washed down with cool white wine and sparkling water. Choose robust metal plates and bowls and plastic cups for on-board dining, and a color scheme of blue and white will look suitably nautical. Pack everything into sturdy baskets and enlist some helpers to carry all the essentials to the pier.

tiny cucumber and egg sandwiches. The food is protected from the hot sun under a canvas cloth stretched from one apple tree to the other. On the side, a large wicker basket is placed to collect presents the guests have brought with them.

The bride and groom have gone on up to the house, where the clans will gather for supper. One long table stretches the whole length of the lawn in front of the house, seating more than one hundred friends and family. Another large table holds the buffet, groaning with tempting dishes. Three kinds of homemade pasta, a whole roast suckling pig, prosciutto and salami, colorful salads, and bowls of fruit make a delightful scene. Finally everyone is seated—but not for long. They soon get up for second helpings and move to other places to greet friends and cousins.

As dusk draws in, the party moves to a grassy knoll behind the house where the bride and groom will cut the cake. Tiny lights come on in the trees over the table; mini flares line the path; torches give light from behind. Everything here is as white as the bride's dress and the five-tiered cake. Champagne is passed to every guest, ready to toast the happy couple after each speech. After the cake is cut, it is handed around on little white napkins. By now darkness has set in, and the evening is rounded off with dancing into the small hours, under the canopy of the starry sky. Another perfect day spent outdoors.

all the modern inventions known to man cannot improve on the flavor of meat, fish, fowl, or vegetables cooked over an open fire

working

Working outdoors offers plenty of scope for creativity—we feel inspired by nature and free to let thoughts roam and ideas develop in the wide open spaces. Everywhere we look, the remarkable organization and beauty of nature should inspire our own creative processes. So, whether it is potting seedlings, writing letters, or studying your accounts, don't let work keep you from the outdoors on a lovely day.

Outdoors, what would otherwise seem like a chore becomes a pleasure. When the sunshine beckons, and you can't resist going out onto the terrace, set up your office in a shady corner. If you use a laptop, you may have trouble seeing the screen, so get a clip-on filter to counter the glare. And how much more relaxing it is to make your phone calls from a quiet corner outside. Alternatively, use this as an escape from screens and phones. Find an easy chair and retire to get through those piles of papers you have been waiting to read, or letters you have been meaning to write. Out here you can clear your mind in the open air, away from ringing phones and e-mails.

If you want to turn your hand to painting, go for a walk and take a box of watercolors and a sketchpad with you. When you come over the brow of a hill and see a picturesque view, a wonderful tree, or gnarled oak, sit down and save it for yourself in a picture. Looking hard at a scene in order to put it down on paper will give you a way of seeing that particular place in detail forever more. If you are a more accomplished artist, and like to paint landscapes or cityscapes in oils, set up your easel and paintbox in front of your view and put down what you see as fast as you can, before the light changes and the shadows lengthen.

Gardening is one of the most satisfying outdoor occupations. Clearing, pruning, planting, and watching plants grow brings out the maternal spirit in us all. On a sunny winter's afternoon, during the thaw, go out to clear up the garden. Plunge into last autumn's leaves and cut back the dead ferns and elephant's ear. New life appears from beneath last year's decay—bulbs already producing bright green shoots, forsythia flowers

with our fingers in the earth, we converse with Mother Nature and feel her elemental forces at work

far left and left **A green-thumbed gardener has all the right equipment: a purpose-built canvas bag has pockets for tools, seed packs, string, and nails; a wooden basket and wide bucket are ideal for carrying plants and cut flowers or taking weeds to the compost pile; rubber clogs are perfect when the earth is muddy; and a wide-brimmed hat provides protection from the sun. And, of course, a comfortable chair made from bent chestnut branches to give your back a well-earned rest.** above right and right **Not all plants need to be in beds. Mixing pots and urns with planted beds offers great flexibility.**

opposite and inset **Why, having gathered colorful flowers from the garden, do you take them into the dark house to arrange? Instead, set up a table in the yard with a variety of pots and vases, some strong shears, and a wire basket for discarded pieces. Use whatever is in bloom and mix in plenty of foliage and berries to create several still lives at the same time, combining colors and sizes. Here you are able to stand back and judge your arrangements in natural light, just as the artist does his canvas.**

this page **Don't take all your cut-flowers indoors, but leave a bucket full of happy yellow sunflowers and marigolds by the front door to welcome guests who are coming over later in the day. Cut flowers add a colorful note to outdoor tables or windowsills, or they might sit unexpectedly on top of a wall. Be sure to put them in heavy pots or metal vases which won't break if they tumble over in the wind or rain.**

gaily yellow, the camellia's elegant blossom in shades of dark red, rose, or white. Japanese cherry suddenly pops into bloom—a lovely surprise on a winter's day, and all the more cherished for being so rare in this leafless season. Rake, clear, prune—cut back the ivy and give the roses climbing space. Later in the spring, it will be time to mow the lawn, plant new shoots, and stake and tie up flowers against the wall. And hard on the heels of the new plants come the weeds and vines, which you must do battle with all summer long.

Use your imagination and energy to engineer new projects in the garden. Why not put in a water garden? There is no upkeep—once you have constructed the pool and put in the plants, your work is done. Water-lilies, nympheas, water hyacinths, and water poppies will constantly change—new buds rise up to the water's surface, faded blossoms sink back down. Put several varieties of colored iris around the edge and hardy bamboos at the back for a wind-break. The water and plants will provide

Create an extra room using a wall of the house or low parapet to define your outdoor space. Plants in pots and climbing over the walls are colorful and ephemeral fill-ins around your chosen spot.
above left and opposite **A metal table and slatted chair make a perfect workspace in a shady nook where the breeze will keep you cool and the plants will keep you calm. This workroom can be quickly transformed into an eating area at lunchtime.**
left **a simple wrought-iron bench with two comfortable cushions makes an inviting seat to take a break from gardening and enjoy a cup of tea.**

constant movement and interest, even on the tiniest plot. Paving stones around the pool can make a level area for a table and chairs.

To make a pretty herb garden and keep it well organized, find the largest cart wheel you can in a local junk shop. Paint it white and lay it down with the hub stuck into the earth and the wheel flush with the ground. Plant different herbs in between the spokes, such as chives, sage, basil, parsley, tarragon, rosemary, and thyme. Pierce the central hub and plant a bushy plant like dark purple lavender. On the edge of the wheel, paint the names of the herbs. And behind your new herb garden, sink a semicircle of cans with both ends removed to contain and control spreaders like mint.

To make an instant garden on a roof terrace or patio where there is no earth, try this recipe. Take one or two bags of topsoil, a selection of terracotta planters (six small, four medium, three large, and one giant), two or three flats of annual flowers, one flat of green plants (like ivy and asparagus fern), and one tree (ideally with spring blossom). Sift the soil into the planters. Plant the flowers and greenery, together. Sprinkle gently with water and place in the sun. For a little shade, set the tree (in the giant planter) near a small outdoor table or bench.

opposite **Move your desk into the sunroom in summer and combine the outdoor world with cut flowers and floral accessories.**
below left **Linger in the sunshine to prepare fruits for the pot and think about all the things you can make with them: desserts and jams, jellies, and preserves. Or you can pop them into plastic bags to put straight into the freezer for use out of season in ice cream.**
below **Pick up nature's hues by using similar colors in your furnishings.**

fill baskets of berries and apples—gathering fruits for the pot is probably the most satisfying of all garden chores

Windows, walls, and doorways can all be brought to life with plants and flowers. Plant a windowbox with ivy and hanging geraniums. Or plant roses, ivy, or clematis in a windowbox on the ground and let them grow up the wall on a trellis or on wires wrapped around strategically placed nails. A doorway can be made more elegant by setting sculpted bushes or balled trees in medium-sized planters, flanking each side of the entrance.

Use existing structures to support flowers and plants. Hanging baskets suspended from wrought-iron hangers will bring an added dimension to a tiny garden. Find a solid beam to put plant hooks into, and remember, your plants will get heavier as they grow, so make sure your balcony, windowsill, roof, or beams can handle what you're going to do with them. And put rollers under big pots before filling them with soil and plants, so you can move them if you need to.

Make sure you can get close enough to your plants to water and take care of them. Inevitably, water will run off and leaves will fall, so give yourself room to get between pots to sweep, and have good catch basins or other ways of dealing with drainage so water run-off

won't annoy your neighbors or cause stains or damage to your building.

Topiary is another way to add interest to a potted or small garden, and is not as difficult to make as you might think. You can buy ready-made frames constructed from green dipped wire or you can bend the wire yourself. Then simply place it in a pot and grow ivy over the wire.

below **Set up your laptop on the terrace on a sunny day to catch up with your correspondence. One advantage of working with a computer is that you don't need to hold down letters with rocks or paperweights. If you do need to use papers, try holding them in a brachial wire holder.**

opposite **The yard makes an excellent outdoor workroom—a carpenter's shop or a place to paint furniture. Painting, with a brush or spray, is a quick way to transform old pieces of furniture—chairs, tables, or beds—from the thrift store into cheerful pieces for indoors or out. Also paint flowerpots to match your outdoor fabrics. Any mess you make will be swept away by the wind and rain.**

furniture

Use creativity and imagination when furnishing your outdoor spaces, drawing on nature's resources—wood, stone, metal—to shape comfortable seats and useful tables. Choose colors, stains, or natural surfaces to suit the mood of the place and blend with surroundings. Walls, paths, ponds, and, of course, trees and flowers are all part of your exterior decorating scheme and should be taken into account.

below right **Today's director's chairs are descendants of eccentric inventions for the camping equipment of yesteryear. Chairs and stools were made with wooden or metal poles and canvas seats and backs that could be packed into the smallest bag.**

below and bottom **Folding chairs are ideal for picnics. Traditionally made from wood and canvas, they come in every color of the rainbow, and modern versions in aluminum are very light and don't rust. Chair seats and backs are made of weather-resistant material that lets the elements through and dries quickly.**

Furniture is essential for life outdoors, and different styles suit different settings. As much in the backyard as in the house, it must be practical, comfortable, and pleasing to the eye.

Position is important—your furniture should focus on the view or provide a space to sit and contemplate a private corner of the space. This is particularly important in the case of stone furniture. Once it is put in place, a stone seat or table is there for life, so think carefully about where you will put it before your furniture

arrives. These monumental pieces last for generations and bring formality and grace to any yard. A statue makes a focal point and gives perspective to a classical garden. A fountain brings life and the refreshing sounds of water to the space. Made from Portland stone, composition marble, or Chilstone, they will be smoothed and weathered by the elements to look as if they have stood there for centuries. Moss and lichen give them a ruddy patina, but they should not be lost under climbing plants.

Intricate and graceful, as well as tough and durable, metal outdoor furniture is a reliable classic. Among the huge variety of ornate shapes and patterns available, iron furniture can be found to suit any style of house or yard. To accommodate variable weather conditions, nineteenth-century cast-iron tables and chairs were made with holes in the surfaces to let rain through. Curved wirework designs have the same effect, but are much lighter than cast iron. An ironwork gazebo is light and airy, and a pretty support for climbing roses or clematis, giving speckled shade to the table and chairs underneath.

Wood, of course, will always blend perfectly in a natural environment, be it the middle of a yard, a park, or shaded by tall trees in a rural landscape. Long-lasting and solid, teak weathers best and eventually takes on a soft gray patina. It is sturdy and can be moved more easily than stone, but once you have planted an oak or teak bench in your yard, it is apt to stay there forever and blend in with the foliage around it.

Wooden furniture can also be stained or painted to enliven a city patio. And a gazebo, with seats and a trellis combined,

above **Some furniture combines metal and wood. French café chairs, for instance, have a sturdy metal frame covered with wooden slats. Give a unity to outdoor space by painting all the furniture one color.**

below **All outdoor furniture can be enhanced with the addition of pillows and blankets brought out from the house to brighten your surroundings and to make your seating more comfortable and decorative.**

makes a romantic spot when covered in vines and totally incorporated into the garden. Adirondack furniture is made from pieces of wood in their natural state, fashioned on the trail by woodsmen on the frontier. In the mountain region that gave this nineteenth-century style its name, chairs and tables were made from branches, knots and all, with wide rush seats or birchbark surfaces.

Another way you can use wood outdoors is with wooden decking. This is an excellent way to extend your living space on a roof terrace or a freestanding area near the pool or the barbecue. Moderately priced and easy to lay, decks provide a warm and flexible surface that is easy to care for and doesn't need mowing! Decks are usually built

above **The fun in outdoor furnishing is making unexpected objects work for you. Here an old cable spool makes an amusing round table on a city terrace.**
above right **A contemporary look is achieved with a slatted bench against a background of a spiky aloe bush. A bright cushion makes a welcome contrast in a mainly green palette.**
right **These sculptured wooden deckchairs weather beautifully and look up-to-date and inviting in a city yard.**

of cedar, teak, or Oroko, the strong and less-expensive eco-alternative to teak. Wet wood will eventually rot, so try to leave a space between the floor and the ground beneath it to filter off rain water. Furnish the area with wooden tables and chairs, and big, colorful cushions.

Wicker is another natural material suited to outdoor furniture. It is reminiscent of the *belle époque*, of potted palms and high teas, when a *meridienne*, a day bed, or a chaise longue graced every Victorian conservatory. Wicker chairs look substantial and inviting, and at the same time are very light to move around. Wicker was developed in French Martinique, a steamy Caribbean island, and should not get too dry, so leave it out on a rainy day to help keep its elasticity. Fashioned in straw reeds or willow shoots, the basketweave design lets the air pass through to keep its occupants cool and comfortable. Indian colonial furniture is in the same family, which we associate with big porches and verandas. These chairs with warm brown wooden frames, and cane or rush seats and backs, have armrests broad enough to accommodate a drink, a book, even your laptop.

below left Two deckchairs are a good solution for a small seating area in the garden: foldable, easily carried indoors, classic in design, but alive with bright-colored stripes. They make an inviting place to relax. **below** An egg-shaped basketchair, round and cozy with a cushion, makes a striking feature, combined with a Chinese lantern and bamboo, in an empty corner of the backyard.

Well-made furniture and fixtures in pure, elemental shapes and materials give a look that will outlast fashion

fabrics

Think of the textures and colors with which nature furnishes her surroundings. She uses every color of the rainbow, changing themes with the seasons, as trees and grasses, flowers and fruits burgeon and surprise us with a shock of color and then die away to the orange and gray of decay. Leaves fall to nourish the earth during another winter, and flowers retreat underground to wait for a new spring.

right **Sugar-pink is a soft color outdoors, and the subdued and faded colors of roses on old-fashioned cotton fabrics blend in with their natural surroundings. A few of these floral pillows on a wicker chair or painted bench make a comfortable and attractive seating area on the porch or lawn.**
below **A faded bolster with a contrasting inset reflects the shadow of bamboo leaves in a corner of the yard.**

When choosing colors for outdoor fabrics, look to nature for inspiration. Sparse bare trees in winter remind us of rough woolen blankets or gray linen. Spring brings a gossamer yellow-green glow to trees and bushes. Tiny flowers push out of bulbs, just sticking their heads above the ground to sniff the arrival of the new season. Gradually all come out of hiding, as nature loses her adolescent delicacy and takes on the full foliage of middle age. Now even the strongest colors and textiles cannot rival her infinite variety. And, as the year draws to a close, the waning months of fall bring the golden colors of retirement.

There are other important points to keep in mind: the strength of the natural light, the landscape surrounding your

space, and the final effect you would like to achieve. If your space is in rural, cool climes, where light is fairly weak, harmonize with your surroundings by choosing fabrics with lots of different shades of green and a few splashes of color. Stick to flowery pastels or a mix of earthy, subdued colors. They will blend in with the landscape, and your decoration will complement, rather than compete with, nature's display.

If you live in a warm climate, you can be a lot more daring. In strong light you can be bold and make a statement with color. Bright pillows can be made from eye-catching African kikoyes or richly colored Indian saris. Recreate a Moroccan terrace with silk velvets and ikats in shades of purple, eggplant, violet, and amethyst, while North African or Native American rugs provide modern verve for floors.

top **Checked tablecloths, napkins, and pillows are traditional and pleasing outdoor linens. Match the colors with handmade pottery to reflect the table's bucolic setting.** above and right **Organza is a light and flowing fabric, and hung alfresco, it makes a pretty see-through curtain, stabilized by a piece of brocade appliquéd to its center. Combine these curtains with matching pillows to define your outside space.**

Traditionally, open air rooms by the ocean or next to swimming pools call for blue fabrics. Stripes are classic, simple and elegant, while turquoise blue and green can be mixed together with great success and will live in complete harmony with the water nearby.

Water-repellent canvas comes in strong, solid or striped colors and makes long-lasting upholstery, awnings, or cushion covers. Again, match the colors and textures to your setting: red and black makes a sophisticated color scheme on a city roof terrace, while a yellow and white awning and yellow canvas pillows look light and bright against a white clapboard house. Old sheets of rough, natural beige linen are also ideal for cushion covers on a contemporary deck—they need nothing more than a contrasting edge, such as fine green piping to give a restrained, elegant look. Ticking is another good outdoor fabric: practical, strong and—in blue, green, or gray—perfect on wooden benches. An old-fashioned linen faded floral cushion matches the mood of a wicker chaise longue. Comfortable pillows in ticking or canvas brighten up iron furniture during the day. Pieces taken from old quilts make attractive pillows for a rocker on a porch, where they were originally made.

left **Red, white, and blue are traditional summer colors that always look fresh and clean. Mix bright blue checks with an old-fashioned floral jaquard fabric and outline a white pique pillow with a bright blue border. The blues are thrown into relief by the red boat pattern on the early American quilt.**
right **On a very modern city terrace, upholstery and pillows make a statement in clean patterns and a simple palette of colors that look good against the river scene in the background. The overall effect makes this a welcome spot to relax with coffee and the papers to enjoy the panoramic view.**

give a finishing touch to your garden decoration with a few treasures brought out from your living room

below Enjoy the last rays of the sun after a busy day's work and take your cup of coffee on a balcony high above the park. The wind can be fierce, but glass panels shelter the seating area and plants outside the penthouse. Pillows are brought out from indoors, and a throw will keep your legs warm. While town and city terraces often call for strong colors, if your setting is a more traditional one, it is wiser to stick to neutrals. White and off-white are always supremely elegant in their simplicity. Variations on the theme can be used in lavish juxtaposition and will look perfect in any setting, complementing the natural palette of wood, sand, or stone. Fabrics can be as rough as canvas or as smooth as an old linen sheet, as airy as cheesecloth, or as transparent as gauze and lace.

lighting

Lighting is the most versatile element in your exterior decorating scheme. You can change the mood in your outdoor rooms with a whim, so use it creatively and redecorate for every occasion. String sparkling electric lights to add a festive air, or use solar lamps to light up your backyard automatically at night. Hang candles inside lanterns from tree trunks, or position them where they will cast reflections on a water feature.

left **An outdoor room needs lighting at night like any other. On this flower-lined terrace, twin lanterns accent the length of the arbor and give it a subtle glow in the evening.**
below **A hurricane lamp decorated with a tangled wreath of leaves looks elegant nestling among the plants.**
bottom **A white embroidered Indian cloth cover for a light or candle swings in the breeze between the climbing vines and the wisteria leaves, bringing an exotic note to your exterior decoration.**

left **A traditional paraffin lamp gives an old-fashioned glow after the sun goes down. Fill it with fuel, light the wick, and cover with a plain or etched glass globe. Position it by the steps from the lawn to light your way in and out of the house.**

below **Candles look wonderful under glass lanterns. These can be hung from the trees above your dining or seating area, from stakes firmly planted in the ground nearby, or from supports screwed into the side of the house.**

The moon and the stars provide natural nighttime illumination outdoors, but they are not always lit up at your convenience! If it is cloudy, or if the moon is dark or just a thin crescent, the night can be very black and sinister. To make the most of your backyard or terrace on a warm evening, you will probably have to provide some of the lighting yourself. Luckily, there is a lighting solution to suit every mood, from permanent wall-mounted electric lights to atmospheric storm lanterns, candles, and flares.

There are all kinds of electric floodlights and beacons that will expand your living area and bathe your yard in light. You can create interesting decorative effects by focusing lights onto an urn against a brick wall, through an arch, or on distant trees.

These low-voltage lights should be made from durable materials, and their cables and transformers well hidden in the foliage. The lights themselves can often be recessed into walls or the ground. If you want to have some backlighting in your flowerbeds or at the base of trees, and you don't have an outdoor electricity supply, try using solar lights, which store up energy all day and automatically light up your plants at night.

A swimming pool offers great opportunities for atmospheric lighting since it will reflect any illuminations you surround it with —perhaps lanterns or miniature stone Japanese temples lit with bulbs or candles. Underwater lights are effective, too, throwing eerie shadows as water and swimmers circulate in the pool.

To create a festive dining area, replace the colored bulbs in mini tree lights with white ones for twinkling summer lighting. String them on the underside of a parasol for a canopy of stars, or hang them from branches to catch the shapes and shadows of textured bark as the tiny bulbs glint and sparkle in the night.

In hot climates you may need well-lit outdoor rooms so you can shift your normal evening activities outside. A porch is ideal, since it has electric outlets that mean you can use normal table lamps by your chair, with special bulbs that keep the bugs away.

For most people, however, an outdoor room has to be lit with the flickering light of a real flame. This is the light reminiscent of clambakes at the beach or camping along the trail, where a campfire provides warmth and a romantic glow after you have finished cooking and encourages conversation far into the night.

the creative use of light and shadow outdoors provides depth and shifting perspective to your nighttime views

this page **Candleholders made from galvanized metal and colored glass will bring an exotic atmosphere to the proceedings. A hanging Moroccan star lantern throws flickering shadows on the table** or floor below. Tiny perforated stars twinkle in the lids of enchanting metal lanterns, which can be laid on the dining table or hung from simple black stakes beside an entrance to welcome your guests.

Closer to home, candles can be lit in lanterns and hung around the yard. Hurricane lamps, with glass covers to protect the flame, are perfect for a dining table, or put one on the sill of each window along the side of the house that is your nocturnal hub of activity. And rows of votive candles in little dishes or pots along a drive or path will give a special welcome to guests as they arrive for a party.

For a more dramatic effect, towering black iron torches on stakes bring a touch of medieval drama to outdoor events. And, to keep insects at bay, light citronella-impregnated flares on bamboo spikes or citronella candles surrounded with decorative shades made from metal mesh.

left **There are many ways to shade outdoor candles from the wind. Here a glass insert is used and held in place with a tiny white picket fence. Mounted on metal spikes, plant several of these candles in flowerpots or straight into the ground around your chairs.**
far left **Colorful Japanese and Chinese paper lanterns give a festive air to the outdoors, suggesting that a party is about to start. They come in many colors and sizes, and look perfect hanging from branches laden with blossom. Light them carefully and then hang them all around the backyard to give a soft gleam among the flowers and trees.**

colorful beach tent

This brightly colored beach tent will provide welcome shelter from the sun and wind during long summer days spent at the beach. It is made from lightweight cotton fabric—muslin, voile, and cheesecloth are ideal—in three different shades. The tent poles and pegs that support the tent are readily available from camping suppliers.

materials and equipment

11 yd. x 45 in. red fabric
10 yd. x 45 in. orange fabric
5 yd. x 45 in. blue fabric
4 tent poles approx. 2 yd. 30 in. long
27 yd. thick string
12 tent pegs
matching sewing thread
tape measure
tailors' chalk
scissors
dressmaker's pins
basting thread and needle
sewing machine
small safety pin

measurements

A = 4 red panels (45 x 90 in.)
B = 4 orange panels (45 x 90 in.)
C = 2 blue panels (45 x 90 in.)
D = 12 red ties (2½ in. x 1 yd.)
E = 4 red loops (2½ x 5 in.)

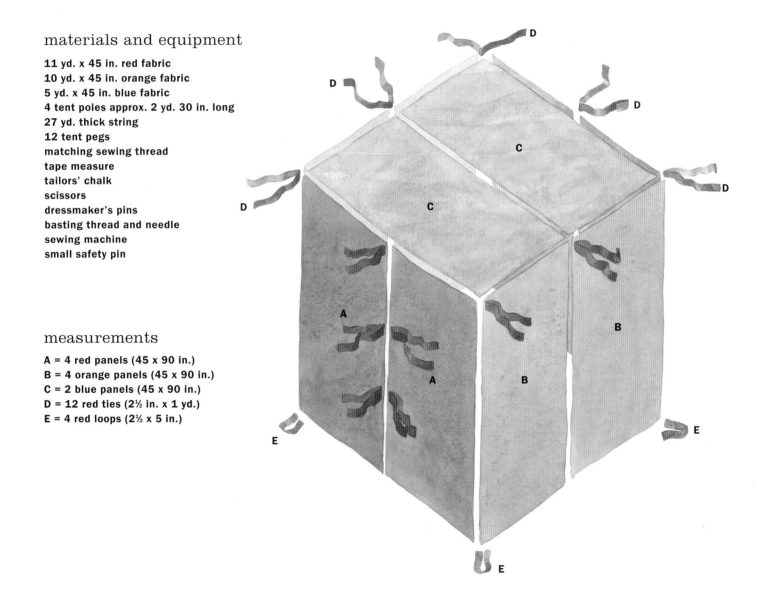

cutting out

1. Following the measurements given opposite, mark the pieces you need on the fabric using tailors' chalk. Then cut out the ten tent panels (four red, four orange and, two blue), twelve ties, and four loops.

to make a French seam

A French seam is a double straight seam that conceals the raw edges on both sides of the fabric. It is a good way to create a neat seam on lightweight fabrics such as voile, organza, or cheesecloth.

a. Pin the two edges to be joined with wrong sides together. Baste, then machine stitch ⅜ in. from the edge (see above). Trim the seam allowance to ¼ in. and press it to one side.

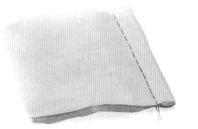

b. Fold right sides together along the stitched line and press, making sure the seam runs along the edge of the fold. Working from the wrong side, pin, baste, and machine stitch ⅜ in. from the fold, enclosing the first seam allowance.

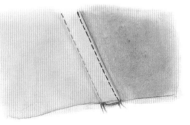

c. Press the new seam allowance to one side and—if you are using a flat French seam—baste it onto the fabric and then machine stitch it down, close to the folded edge.

making the tent

2. Finish one selvedge on two of the red panels with a ⅜ in. double hem: press under ⅜ in., then a further ⅜ in. (see below). Pin, baste, then machine stitch along the inner fold. These panels will form the front of the tent.

3. Using flat French seams (see page 121), sew the other two red panels together to make the back, and join the orange panels in pairs to make the sides. In the same way, stitch the side pieces to the back and join the unhemmed edges of the front to the side pieces (see below). Run a double hem along the bottom.

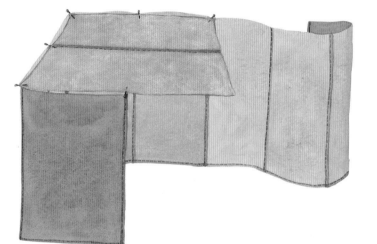

4. Again using a flat French seam, join the two blue panels to make the roof. Using tailors' chalk, mark the midpoint of each side edge.

5. With wrong sides together, pin the walls to the roof. Start by matching the corner of one front panel to the midpoint of one roof edge, then pin the seam to the corner. Pin the next two seams together, then continue working around the roof piece, pinning seams and corners as they meet (see left). Join the walls and roof using a French seam. Press the enclosed seam allowance toward the roof, then turn right side out.

making the ties and loops

6. The ties and loops are made in the same way. Fold the strip in half lengthwise with right sides together, then pin and baste the two long edges together. Machine stitch ¼ in. from the edge, then attach a safety pin to one open end. Feed the pin back through the tube to turn the fabric right side out (see right).

7. Finish the ends by pressing under a ⅜ in. turning. Finish off by machine stitching around the edge of the tie ⅛ in. from the outside (see below).

8. Fold eight of the ties in half. Attach to the corners and midpoints of the roof with stab stitch, sewing through the seam allowance to make them secure (see below). With tailors' chalk, make two equally spaced marks on each side of the front opening and stitch the remaining four ties to these points to make the fastening.

9. Fold the loops in half and stitch the two ends of each one to a bottom corner of the tent (see left).

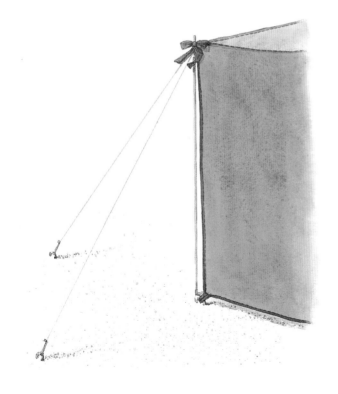

erecting the tent

10. To make the guy ropes, cut the string into four equal lengths and tie a slip knot at both ends of each piece.

11. Push the four tent poles firmly into the sand, one at each corner. Tie the corners of the roof to the top of the tent poles in tight bows, and anchor the bottom corners with tent pegs at the foot of each post. Place the guy ropes over the points of the poles and stretch out the ends at an angle to the tent. Peg the loops into the sand (see left). The tent can be kept open by tying the front panels back to the tent poles.

decorative chair cover

A set of traditional folding café chairs can be dressed up for a summer garden party in these billowing covers with full, gathered skirts, tied in place at the back with a sashlike bow. They are simply made from a series of rectangles cut from plain cotton voile or any similar transparent fabric. No pretense here—you can see the frame of the chair through the material.

materials and equipment

**closely woven sheer fabric
(approx. 3¼ yd. x 60 in.)
matching sewing thread
tape measure
squared pattern paper
pencil and long ruler
scissors
dressmaker's pins
basting thread and needle
sewing machine**

making the pattern and cutting out

1. Following the diagrams (see right and opposite) and the measurements given below, draw the six main pieces, plus the four strips for the ties, full scale on pattern paper. Add a seam allowance of ⅝ in. around each shape and cut out. Check the accuracy of the pattern against the chair and make any necessary adjustments.

A = inside back (width = p + 1¼ in.; depth = q)
B = seat (top width = r; bottom width = s; depth = t)
C = front skirt (width = 2 x s; depth = u)
D = 2 side skirts (width = 2 x t; depth = u)
E = outside back (width = p + 14 in.; depth = q + u)
F = 4 ties (width = 30 in.; depth = 6 in.)

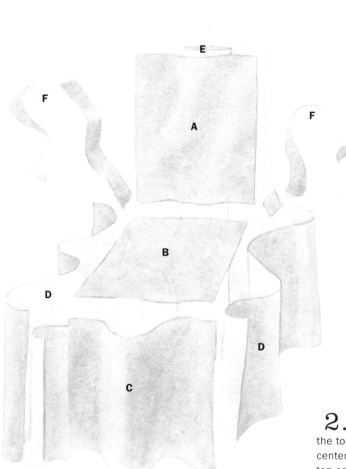

2. Lay the pattern pieces out on the fabric so the grain runs from the top to bottom. Pin in place, then cut out. Cut notches to mark the center points on each edge of B, the top and bottom edges of A, and the top edges of E, C, and both D pieces. Press and label each piece.

to make the gathers

Fabric can quickly be gathered into folds, using two rows of machine stitch. The stitch length should be adjusted to its longest setting and the top tension loosened so the bobbin (underside) threads can be pulled up easily.

a. Working from the right side, sew a row of straight stitch ¼ in. from the edge to be gathered, then stitch a second row ¼ in. below the first. Leave long threads at both ends of the stitching.

b. With the wrong side of the fabric uppermost, carefully pull the two bobbin threads, working from each end in turn. Ease the fabric toward the center a little at a time (see below), until the gathers are approximately the right length.

making the skirt and seat

1. Using a French seam (see page 121), join the top edge of the seat to the lower edge of the inside back. Again using French seams, attach one side edge of each side skirt to the side edges of the front skirt. Press the fabric to remove any creases.

2. Make two rows of gathering stitches (see page 125) along the top edge of the skirt. Start at the top corner and divide the stitches into six sections, breaking off and starting again at the three notches and on each side of the two vertical seams (see right). Do not stitch into the seam allowance at each end of the skirt.

3. With right sides together, pin the skirt to the seat, matching the notches along the top of the skirt to the notches on the seat, the seams of the skirt to the corners of the seat, and the corners of the skirt to the seam at the top edge of the seat (see left).

4. Pull up the bobbin threads (see page 125) so that each gathered section fits approximately along the edge to which it is pinned.

5. To secure each gathered section, insert a pin at one end of the stitches and anchor the loose threads by winding them around the pin. Pull up the other two threads and gently ease the fabric until the gathers are the exact length (see right). Then anchor them with another pin.

6. Adjust the folds so the fullness is distributed evenly along the skirt. Pin the two edges together, right sides together, and baste firmly, using small stitches to keep the gathers in place (see right). Return the machine settings to normal, and machine stitch slowly over the gathers, following the seam line. Trim the seam allowance and finish with a row of zigzag or overlock stitch. Snip off any loose threads and press.

making the back

7. To make the inverted pleat at the top edge of the outside back, clip two notches, each 6 in. from the center notch. Line them up to the center and pin the folds in place (see right). Work a line of basting across the top of the pleat.

8. With wrong sides together, pin and baste the side edges of the inside back and the side skirts to the outside back (see left). Clip into the seam allowance between the seat and the inside back so the seam will lie flat.

9. Turn the other way out and complete the French seams (see right). Make another French seam to join the top edges of the inside and outside back, and press.

making the ties

10. Join the long edges of two tie strips together with French seams. Make another French seam to finish off one short end (see below), and press. Follow the same method for the second tie.

11. Fold under and press the raw edge of the unfinished end, then gather (see page 125) it up to a width of 2½ in. Slipstitch to the seam line at the lower edge of the inside back (see above). Make and attach the second tie in the same way.

12. Turn under and press a ⅜ in. double hem along the lower edge of the cover. Baste, then machine stitch close to the inside fold. Finally, slip the cover over the chair and make the ties into a loose bow at the back to keep it in place.

floral tablecloth

Making this tablecloth is a practical way to use up remnants of floral chintz, gingham, and other printed furnishing fabrics. It is made from four striped triangles that create a pattern of concentric squares. Although the selection of fabrics in this example appears random, it is limited to three main colors—pink, blue, and cream—which gives cohesion and unity to the overall design.

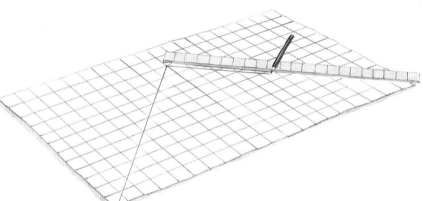

materials and equipment

selection of fabric
white sewing thread
squared pattern paper
pencil and long ruler
scissors
tailors' chalk
basting thread and needle
sewing machine

making the template

1. Mark a triangle on the pattern paper. Draw a baseline 60 in. long, mark the midpoint and draw a 30 in. line at right angles. Add two lines joining the ends of the baseline to the top of the shorter line (see above), then cut out the template.

making the triangles

2. Cut four strips of fabric measuring 4 x 60 in. each. These will form the border of the tablecloth. Fold each strip in half widthwise and mark the centre with tailors' chalk. Cut four strips measuring 4 x 53⅜ in. from contrasting fabric to make the next round. Mark the midpoints.

3. With right sides together, pin and baste one long and one shorter strip together, matching the chalk marks (see above). Machine stitch ⅜ in. from the edge, then finish the raw edges with an overlock stitch or zigzag. Press the seam allowance toward the longer strip. Join the other strips in pairs the same way.

4. The next four strips are 4 x 47¼ in. Cut out, mark the centers, and sew to the previous strips as before. Continue adding strips of fabric (see above), reducing the length by 6⅜ in. each time, until each triangle is complete, with ten stripes. You can vary the width of the strips slightly to give variety.

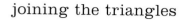

joining the triangles

5. Pin the paper template to a finished triangle, lining up the long edges, and cut out the fabric (see left). Cut out the other three pieces the same way.

6. With right sides together, pin two triangles to each other along one short edge, carefully matching the seams. Baste and machine stitch, leaving a ⅜ in. seam allowance. Finish the raw edges and press the seam to one side. Join the other two triangles the same way. Pin the two large triangles along the longest edge to make the square. Baste, machine stitch, finish the seam, then press the allowance flat (see below).

finishing

7. To finish the edge, press under a ⅜ in. hem around the border, then press the border in half so the folded edge lines up with the first seam.

8. Finish each corner with a miter. Unfold the deeper turning and fold the corner over at an angle of 45 degrees so the creases line up to form a right angle.

9. Refold the turnings, press lightly, and pin the fold to the wrong side, so it conceals the first seam allowance. Baste in place, then slipstitch the two sides of each miter together, starting at the point and working inward. Handstitch the hem to the cloth, sewing through the seam allowance so the stitches do not show through on the right side. Press the hem.

garden settle

This pleasing traditional design is made using very modern methods, which make it possible to construct the bench in a weekend. The pieces can all be cut from one standard-size sheet of plywood. Particle boards such as Medium Density Fibreboard (MDF) or chipboard will not do, because the edges will not take screws or nails and these boards are not waterproof. Exterior-grade plywood is good, but marine-grade plywood is best. Some have decorative top veneers, which are very attractive. Homecenters and lumberyards are good sources of exterior-grade materials. The power tools needed can be rented. Rented tools are generally of better quality than home workshop tools and consequently produce better results. They should also be supplied with sharp industrial-quality blades. Always wear ear plugs and goggles when using powersaws and a dust mask if you are working indoors.

materials and equipment

4 x 8 ft., ¾ in.-thick plywood
2 in. ring-barbed nails
waterproof wood glue
primer and exterior enamel paint
pencil and long ruler
wooden battens for supports and guides
portable circular saw
clamps
portable jigsaw
drill, with ⅛ in. bit
power sander or sandpaper
masking tape
hammer

marking and cutting out

1. Draw the parts listed below on the plywood as shown opposite. Use a long straightedge for the straight lines and full-size paper patterns or a grid marked on the plywood to mark the curves. You will need enough workspace to allow the board to be laid flat on wood battens with room for you to move around for measuring and cutting.

A and B = side pieces
C = back
D = seat
E = front rail

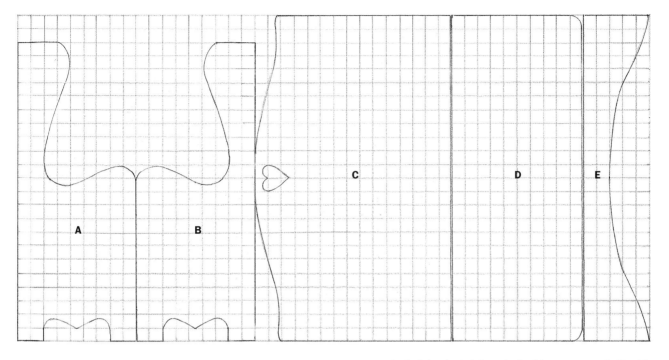

A   B   C   D   E

standard-size sheet of plywood = 8 x 4 ft.; one square of grid = 2 in.

2. The straight edges are cut first with a portable circular saw (see right). To cut accurately to the required line, set up a straight wooden batten, clamped to the plywood. This needs to be offset from the marked line by the distance of the blade from the edge of the base of the saw. Check this two or three times to insure correct positioning before committing to a cut. It is worth taking the time to get this right as the sawn edge will be straight and square and needs no further preparation. Make sure the work is supported by battens on each side of the cut and adjust the saw blade to penetrate just to the depth of the plywood.

3. A portable jigsaw is used for the curves (see right). Here the quality of the plywood comes into play. Better plywoods have a stronger bond between the laminates, making breakout less pronounced around cuts. It is also important to use sharp and fairly fine blades. Smaller teeth on the blade will produce a slower cut but a finer finish. A drilled hole in the heart-shaped cutout will enable entry to begin cutting out with the jigsaw.

4. Curved edges can now be rounded over and sanded smooth, either with a power sander or by hand. This will make the settle comfortable and prevent wear in use.

assembling the settle

5. Ring-barbed nails are stronger than conventional nails and are used here in conjunction with waterproof wood glue for assembly. The positions of the joints are marked and masked off with masking tape to protect the surrounding work from unwanted glue. The tape also provides a guide for drilling pilot holes. These should be about ⅛ in. in diameter and go through the first part of the joint only. The principle purpose of the pilot holes is to guide the nail square into the joint (see below).

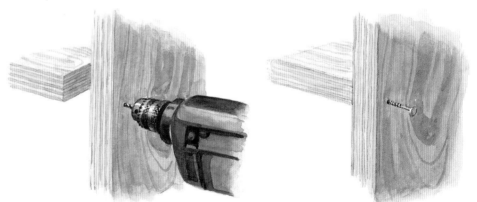

6. The seat is set on the bottom edge of the back and top edge of the front rail (see right). Mask off and predrill the nail positions along the front and back of the seat. It is vital that the sides of the front rail, seat and back line up—this can be done by tacking overhanging strips of wood to each end of the seat, which can be pulled off after assembly.

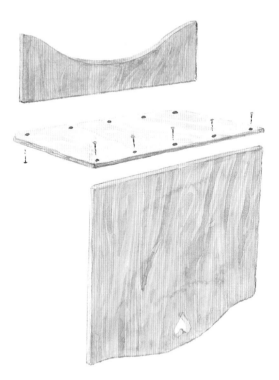

7. The back must be secured in a vise or held by a helper to allow for accurate alignment of the seat. Apply glue to both surfaces of the joint and (especially on the edge of the plywood) allow it to soak in for a few minutes before applying a second coat and removing the tape. Press the surfaces together and secure with nails. Turn the assembly over to fit the front rail in the same way (see right). Wipe off any excess glue with a damp cloth.

8. To fit the ends (see left), again mask off and predrill the nail positions before gluing and nailing. This becomes easier as the structure nears completion.

finishing

9. Sand and round over any exposed edges and prime all the edges with a coat of glue. The edges of plywood are highly absorbent and priming will make them more waterproof and easier to paint.

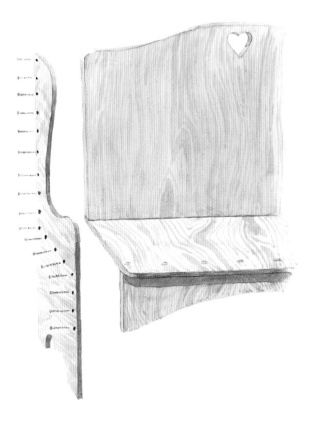

10. If you are proud of your work and a decorative veneered plywood was chosen, the piece could be finished with marine-grade varnish, though this is recommended only if the piece is to be kept under cover. For painting, prime and apply two coats of exterior enamel.

nesting box

A nesting box is an enjoyable feature in any backyard. This traditional design is built using modern methods, making it very simple to construct. Only half a sheet of standard-sized exterior-grade plywood is required, unless you want to make two! The box illustrated here has a roof tiled with shells. You may have other ideas for customizing the project, such as cutting roofing felt into "shales" and tacking them on or using ceramic tiles in a mosaic.

material and equipment

4 x 4 ft., ¾ in.-thick exterior-grade plywood
7 ft.-long straight branch or 4 x 4 in. post
(allows for bottom 2 ft. to be set into the ground)
1¼ in. ring-barbed nails
exterior wood glue and paint
pencil and long ruler
circular saw
jigsaw
electric drill with hole-cutter
hand plane and sandpaper

marking and cutting out

1. Draw the parts by marking a grid on the plywood (see right). Cut them out by following the straight drawn lines freehand with a circular saw. The angles on the top edges of the roof components are cut with the saw set at 45 degrees so they fit together neatly at the roof ridge. The components for the post bracket, the roof ridge, and the cutouts on the base and front are too small to be safely cut in this way, and a jigsaw should be used. The hole at the top of the front is best cut with a hole-cutter in an electric drill. All the edges need planing with a hand plane, and the cutouts should be sanded smooth.

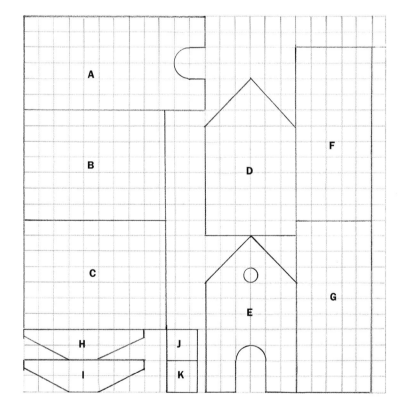

sheet of ply = 4 x 4 ft.
one square of grid = 2 in.

A = base
B and C = sides
D = back
E = front
F and G = roof pieces
H and I = post bracket sides
J and K = post bracket spacers

assembling the box

2. Assembly begins with the post bracket (see right). The widths of the spacers and their positions on the side pieces are marked on the post itself, allowing just enough tolerance for fitting. Using a vise will aid assembly, so that nails can be accurately driven through the side pieces into the spacers.

3. Next the bracket is positioned on the base of the box (see left). The positions of the nails must be carefully marked before nailing since the nails are driven from the upper side of the base and can easily miss their mark.

4. The front, back, and sides are assembled next (see right). Hold one side in a vise and nail one edge of the back piece to it. Arrange the opposite side in the same way and repeat. The assembly can be rested on the floor to fit the final end.

5. To fit the base, the box construction is inverted. This needs to be supported on a couple of thick battens or two rolled-up blankets to protect the ridge of the roof and keep the job steady while nailing (see below).

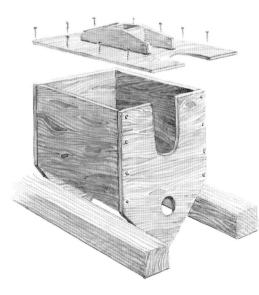

6. Turn the bird box the right way up and again make sure it is properly supported before nailing the roof pieces in position (see below).

finishing

7. Any rough edges should be sanded smooth and the outer surfaces given two sealing coats of dilute exterior wood glue to prime them for painting. The inside of the box should not be sealed or painted because the finish may be toxic to wildlife. The post is painted with wood preserver before being set into the ground. Finally, the box is nailed to the post through the bracket.

rustic stool

This simple project could serve as a table, a stand for a potted plant, or a seat. The materials may be readily available to you or can, alternatively, be acquired from a tree surgeon or landscape contractor. The diameter of the top could be adjusted to anything from 6 inches for a small stand to 2—2½ feet for a table. 1—1½ feet is ideal for the seat shown here. When choosing logs for the legs, select a thickness that will balance visually with the depth of the top.

materials and equipment

**bark-covered log (1—1½ ft. diameter and
    approx. 2 in. thick to provide strength
    without undue bulkiness)**
waterproof wood glue
log for the stool's legs
ring-barbed nails
parcel tape
chisel
pruning or woodworking saw
drill
hammer

1. If you wish to retain the bark, which will probably fall off with time, it is as well to strip it off at this stage and glue it back on. Prime both surfaces to be bonded with glue, let it dry, and then apply wet glue to one surface and tape the bark back in position with parcel tape (see below). When the glue is dry, remove the tape and pare off any excess glue with a sharp chisel.

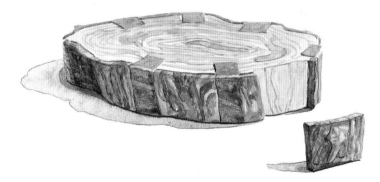

2. Saw the legs to a suitable length (approx. 1½ x diameter of the top) at an angle of 45 degrees using a pruning or woodworking saw (see below). The saw should be dried after use; otherwise, the moisture in the branch will cause it to rust.

assembling the legs

3. The ring-barbed nails you use should be nearly twice the thickness of the legs in length (long enough to make a good joint without coming out of the other side). Holes are drilled to slightly less than the diameter of the nail through the top ends of the legs where they will be joined to the seat (see right). The ends of the legs will be liable to splitting if nails are driven through without a pilot hole.

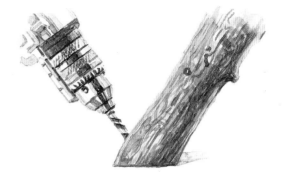

4. The first stage of assembly is nailing two of the legs together to form a cross (see left). The legs need to be set so the feet will rest flat on the ground and the top ends will butt onto the seat. Place the legs roughly in position on the upturned top to gauge the position of the joint. Unseasoned wood is wet and unlikely to split when nailing (except at the ends), so a pilot hole is probably not necessary.

5. The position of the third leg is again gauged by arranging the feet flat on the ground. Nail the third leg to one of the other two (see below). Make sure the frame is well supported before nailing, both for safety and to prevent damage to the first joint.

attaching the seat

6. There should be enough play in the leg assembly to allow the frame to be set up, resting fairly flat on the inverted seat. The pilot holes drilled earlier will help guide the nails and prevent the leg assembly from being pushed out of alignment while you hammer the legs in place (see right).

sources

SUPPLIERS AND DESIGNERS WHOSE
PRODUCTS AND WORK ARE FEATURED
IN THIS BOOK

Albrizzi
Via Bagutta 8
Milan
Italy
(39) 02-76001218
Hand-bound stationery

Anthropologie
375 West Broadway
New York, NY
(212) 343-7070 for branches
www.anthropologie.com
**Reproduction decorative hardware,
Moroccan lanterns, bamboo folding
recliners**

La Boutique des Jardins
1 Cours Mirabeau
13210 St Remy-de-Provence
France
(33) 04-90921160
**Garden furniture, home and fashion
accessories**

Boutique du Club 55
Plage de Pampelonne
43 Boulevard Patch
Ramatuelle 83350
France
(33) 04-94798014
Beachwear

Chez Juju
Plage de Beaduc
Camargue 13
France
Fish restaurant

La Compagnia Coloniale
Via Torino 68
Milan
Italy
(39) 02-8052746
**Travel and adventure-ware and
accessories**

La Compagnia dell'Oriente
Via S. Marta 10
20122 Milano
Italy
(39) 02-89013087
**Antique Chinese furniture, decorative
and fashion accessories**

The Conran Shop
407 East 59th Street
New York, NY10022
(212) 755-9079
www.conran.com

Coté Bastide
3 Rue du Grand Pré
84160 Lourmarin
France
(33) 04-90085792
Toiletries and bath accessories

Crate & Barrel
1860 West Jefferson Avenue
Naperville, IL 60540
**For a store near you,
call (800) 927-9202**
www.crateandbarrel.com
**Outdoor dinnerware, furniture, and
accessories**

Flore Derenne Brocante
**Marché à la Brocante de L'Isle sur
Sorgue 84800**
France
(Sunday mornings)
(33) 04-90383954
Country antiques

Galerie Afrique
Rue de Sarrasins
Ramatuelle
France
(33) 01-43972949–494792075
African antiques, jewelry, textiles

Galeries Tropeziennes
56 Rue Gambetta
83990 Saint Tropez
France
(33) 04-94970221
Houseware, tableware, textiles

Garden Images Limited
15 Meer Street
Stratford Upon Avon
CV37 6QB
UK
**For mail order,
call (44) 01564 794035**
www.garden-images.co.uk
Tools and accessories for gardeners

Pierre and Sandrine De Grugiller
Le Mas de Flore
Lagnes 84800
France
(33) 04-90203796
Antique and made-to-order furniture

Habitat
196 Tottenham Court Road
London W1P 9LD
UK
(44) 0645 334433 for branches
www.habitat.net
Furnishings and accessories

Carolina Herrera
954 Madison Avenue
New York, NY
Fashion retail

Hoepli bookshop
Via Hoepli
Milan
Italy
(39) 02-864871
Bookstore

Dale Loth Architects
1 Cliff Road
London NW1 9AJ
UK
(44) 020 7485 4003
(44) 020 7284 4490
mail@dalelotharchitects.ltd.uk

Nicoletta Marazza Design
Milan 20121
Italy
(by appointment)
(39) 02-76014482
Interior designer

Minh Mang
182 Battersea Park Road
London SW11 4ND
UK
020 7498 3233
Asian fabrics and accessories

Pearl River Chinese Products
277 Canal Street
New York, NY
(212) 219-8107
Fashion and home accessories

Claudia Pellegatta
Milan
Italy
(by appointment)
(39) 02-58300589

Carla Saibene
Via della Spiga 46
20121 Milan
Italy
(39) 02-77331570
Fashion designer

Saunderskill Farms
Accord, NY
(914) 626-2676
**Garden nurseries, home-farm
producers and retailers**

L'Utile e il Dilettevole
Via Della Spiga 46
20121 Milan
Italy
(39) 02-76004820
www.utile-dilettevole.it
Antique furniture, garden furniture,
decorative objects, soft furnishings,
textiles

Claude Vacherot
L'Ile aux Brocantes
L'Isle sur Sorgue 84800
France
(33) 04-90619720
Antiques

White on White
888 Lexington Avenue
New York NY
Gustavian furniture, nordic-style
home, table, bed accessories,
mainly white

FURNISHINGS AND ACCESSORIES

ABC Carpet & Home
777 South Congress
Delray Beach, FL
For a store near you,
call (561) 279-7777
www.abchome.com
Furniture, tableware, fabrics,
accessories

Laura Ashley
398 Columbus Avenue
New York, NY 10024-5105
(212) 496-5110

Barneys
660 Madison Avenue
New York, NY
(212) 826-8900
www.barneys.com

Bed, Bath and Beyond
620 6th Avenue
New York, NY 10011
For a store near you,
call (800) GOBEYOND
www.bedbathandbeyond.com
Outdoor dinnerware, furniture, and
accessories

Bloomingdales
1000 Third Avenue
New York, NY10022
(212) 705-2000
www.bloomingdales.com

Giata Designs
614 Santa Barbara Street
Santa Barbara, CA 93101
(805) 965-6535
Fabric used outdoors for patio
furniture, umbrellas, and awnings

Grange Furniture
200 Lexington Avenue
New York, N.Y. 10016
(212) 685-9057
Reproduction French furniture,
wicker, painted furniture, garden
furnishings

Homecrest
Box 350
Wadena, MN 56482
(888) 346-4852
www.homecrest.com
Outdoor furniture

IKEA
Potomac Mills Mall
2700 Potomac Circle
Suite 888
Woodbridge, VA 22192
For a store near you,
call (800) 254-IKEA
www.ikea.com

Lack's Outdoor Furniture
P.O. Box 2365
Myrtle Beach, SC 29578-2365
(800) 455-2257
www.sscoast.net/lacks

Ralph Lauren Home Collection
1185 Avenue of the Americas
New York, NY 10036
For a retailer near you,
call (212) 642-8700

Penine Hart
457 Broome Street
New York, NY 10012
(212) 226-2761
Antique country furniture, Indian
pillows, blankets from Madrid, garden
ornaments

Pier 1 Imports
499 Tarrytown Road
White Plains, NY 10607
For a store near you, call
(800) 44-PIER1
www.pier1.com
Wicker, rattan, reed and bamboo
furniture, country-style furniture,
baskets, candles, candleholders,
dinnerware, accessories

Pottery Barn
P.O. Box 7044
San Francisco, CA 94120-7044
For a store near you,
call (800) 922-9934
www.potterybarn.com
Outdoor dinnerware, furniture,
accessories

Smith & Hawken
117 East Strawberry Drive
Mill Valley, CA 94941
For a store near you,
call (800) 776-3336
www.smithandhawken.com
Adirondack chairs, outdoor furniture,
accessories

Sunbrella Fabrics
Glen Raven Mills Inc.
1831 N. Park Ave.
Glen Raven, NC 27217
(336) 227-6211
www.sunbrella.com
Fabric used outdoors for patio
furniture, umbrellas, and awnings

Vermont Outdoor Furniture
9 Auburn Street
Barre, VT 05641
(800) 588-8834
www.vermontoutdoorfurnitur.com
Cedar furniture for the outdoors

Williams-Sonoma
51 Highland Park Village
Dallas Highland
Dallas, TX 75205
For a store near you,
call (800) 541-2233
www.williamssonoma.com

GARDEN ACCESSORIES

American Designer Pottery
13612 Midway Road, Suite 200
Dallas, TX 75244
(888) 388-0319
www.amdesignerpottery.com
Gardening and outdoor accessories

L. Becker Flowers
217 East 83rd Street
New York, N.Y. 10028
(212) 439-6001
RCFurn@aol.com
Unique garden-related antiques,
furniture, pots, urns

Charleston Gardens
61 Queen Street
Charleston, SC 29401
(800) 469-0118
www.charlestongardens.com
Stepping stones, garden ornaments,
lighting, fountains, furniture

Harry & David's Northwest Express
Northwest Express
P.O. Box 1548
Medford, OR 97501-0400
(800) 727-7243
www.northwestexpress.com
Birdfeeders

Kinsman Company
River Road
Point Pleasant, PA 18950-0357
(800) 396-1251
www.kinsmangarden.com
Container gardens

Lexington Gardens
1011 Lexington Avenue
New York, N.Y. 10021
(212) 861-4390
Antique and new garden furniture and
accessories

LL Bean
95 Main Street
Freeport, ME 04032-9967
(800) 453-0340
www.llbean.com
Barbecues, outdoor games, toys,
backyard accessories, lanterns

The New York Botanical Garden
200th St. & Southern Blvd.
Bronx, NY 10458
(718) 817-8700
www.nybg.org
Gardening and outdoor accessories

Restoration Hardware
15 Koch Road, Suite J
Corte Madera, CA 94925
For a store near you,
call (800) 816-0969
www.restorationhardware.com
Potting bench, garden accessories

Treillage Ltd.
418 East 75th Street
New York, NY 10021
(212) 535-2288
Antique garden furniture, terracotta
pots, gardening equipment

Walpole Woodworkers
767 East Street
Walpole, MA 02081
(800) 343-6948
www.walpolewoodworkers.com
Furniture, childlife play systems,
lamp posts, signs, and mailboxes

GARDENING PRODUCTS

All-America Rose Selections
221 N. LaSalle Street
Chicago, IL 60601
(312) 372-7090
www.rose.org
Roses

American Standard Company
157 Water Street
Southington, CT 06489
(800) 275-3618
www.florianratchetcut.com
Gardening tools

Burpee
002717 Burpee Lane
Warminster, PA 18974
(800) 888-1447
www.burpee.com
Seeds, plants

Champion of Indianapolis
8461 Castlewood Drive
Indianapolis, IN 46250
(800) 866-6301
www.championwindows.com
Windows, patio rooms

Home Depot
2455 Paces Ferry Road
Atlanta, GA 30339
For a store near you,
call (800) 430-3376
www.homedepot.com

Vixen Hill
Dept. WD-9
Main Street
Elverson, PA 19520
(800) 423-2766
www.vixenhill.com
Gazebos, gardenhouses, pavilions

OUTDOOR LIGHTING

Aladdin Industries
703 M-Boro Road
Nashville, TN 37210
(800) 251-4535
Oil and kerosene lamps

Beachside Lighting
127-A Hekili Street
Kailua, HI 96734
(808) 263-5717
www.beachsidelighting.com
Landscape lighting fixtures, tiki
torches

Islecraft
P.O. Box 217
Beaver Island, MI 49782
(231) 448-2977
www.islecraft.com
Citronella candles

Landscape Lighting Co.
4 Chip Lane
Reading, PA 19607
(610) 796-7844
Outdoor lighting

Stonce Lighting
120 East Gloucester Pike
Barrington, NJ 08007
(856) 546-5500
www.stoncolighting.com
Outdoor lighting

BARBECUES

Broilmaster
301 East Tennessee Street
Florence, AL 35631
For a retailer near you,
call (800) 255-0403
www.broilmaster.com
Grills, accessories

Fireplace & Patio Unlimited
8200 Louisiana Street
Merrillville, IN 46410
(219) 769-3473
www.fireplacepatiounl.com
Gas grills, outdoor furniture,
accessories

Weber-Stephen Products Co.
200 East Daniels Road
Palatine, IL 60067-6266
For a retailer near you,
call (800) 446-1071
www.weber.com
Grills, accessories

picture credits

Key: t = top, b= below, l = left,
r = right, c = center

1: Enrica Stabile's house in Provence.
2: La Bastide Rose, Nicole & Pierre Salinger's house, Le Thor, France; checked pillows, tablecloth, awning, baskets, & plates, L'Utile e il Dilettevole; blue thermos & blue cheese grater, Habitat; blue glasses, La Boutique des Jardins. **3**: **l** mattresses & children's chair, L'Utile e il Dilettevole; Chinese baby shoes, La compagnia dell'Oriente. Thank you to Andrea Pigato; **c** white umbrella, Coté Bastide; deckchair, Habitat; hamman towel, Galeries Tropeziennes; aluminum sun mattress& silver flask bag, La Compagnia Coloniale; **r** marbleized pitcher & blue latticed shelf, L'Utile e il Dilettevole. **4**: cotton pareo, Club 55. **5**: cotton muslin beach hut, canvas cot, & raffia mattress, L'Utile e il Dilettevole; blue indigo throw, Galerie Afrique. **6**: Bill & Randie Fiucci's house in Upstate New York; tartan plaid, L'Utile e il Dilettevole. **7**: **l** Joel & Yuta Powell's house in the Hudson River Valley; linen checked napkins, L'Utile e il Dilettevole; **r** plates & golden bowl, Anthropologie; tablecloth, L'Utile e il Dilettevole. **8**: **l**, **tr** a Soho rooftop, New York; straw mat & Chinese paper lantern, L'Utile e il Dilettevole; tea set & bolster, Anthropologie; **br** Enrica Stabile's house in Provence; tablecloth, creamware teacup, & pillow, L'Utile e il Dilettevole. **9**: Enrica Stabile's house in Provence; pillow & throw, L'Utile e il Dilettevole; glass, Habitat. **12 & 13**: La Bastide Rose, Nicole & Pierre Salinger's house, Le Thor, Provence; iron bed, garden chair, tin candlestick, cotton bag, antique bedspread, & pillows, L'Utile e il Dilettevole; mosquito net, La Boutique des Jardins; storm lantern, Le Mas de Flore; straw slippers, Minh Mang. **14**: linen pillow, L'Utile e il Dilettevole; wicker tray, pitcher, & glass, Habitat; pareo & straw hat, Boutique Club 55. **15**: lace curtains, white pillow, zinc basin & pitcher, & folding stool, L'Utile e il Dilettevole; iron & glass wall sconce, Nicoletta Marazza. **16 & 17**: Liliane Dexemple's house, Le Thor, Provence; wicker chaise longue & blue sun shade, Claude Vacherot; pillow,

straw flask, & cotton throw, L'Utile e il Dilettevole. **18 & 19**: **l** bench, pillows, pottery pitcher, baskets, watering can, & lattice shelf, L'Utile e il Dilettevole; deckchair & garden pots, Claude Vacherot; **r** chestnut table, majolica, & wire basket, L'Utile e il Dilettevole. **20 & 21**: Enrica Stabile's house, Le Thor, Provence; Cornishware teacup & printed pillows, L'Utile e il Dilettevole. **22**: Joel & Yuta Powell's house in the Hudson River Valley; chicken in the basket & red quilt, Yuta Powell's Americana collection. **23**: Joel & Yuta Powell's house in the Hudson River Valley; quilted pillow, l'Utile e il Dilettevole. **24**: La Bastide Rose, Nicole & Pierre Salinger's house, Le Thor, Provence; striped mattress, cotton herringbone throw, & pillow, L'Utile e il Dilettevole. **25**: mattress, throw, & pillow, as above; fishing gear, basket, & oars, Clad Vacherot. **26 & 27**: Guido & Marilea Somaré's house, Milan; old paper box & papers, Marilea Somaré. **28**: Thank you to Soliane Burg, Karin Kern, Capucine Schnell, & Roger Schnell; gypsy wagon from Eleveur de Chevaux de Trait, 84320 Entraigues-sur-Sorgues. **29**: Jara's Equine center, Kerhonkson, NY; tartan plaid & jacket, Carolina Herrera. **30**: Sunderskill Farms, Accord, NY; glasses in straw holders, Habitat. **31**: Joel & Yuta Powell's house in the Hudson River Valley; **r** Sunderskill Farms, Accord, NY. **32**: Bill & Randie Fiucci's house in upstate New York; Adirondack arbor made by owners; pillows, L'Utile e il Dilettevole. **33**: Joel & Yuta Powell's house in the Hudson River Valley; bench, rocking horse, mamie dolls, & spongeware pitcher, Yuta Powell's Americana collection; pillow, L'Utile e il Dilettevole. **34 & 35**: Giorgio & Irene Silvagni's house in Provence; sofa bed by Giorgio Silvagni by order from L'Utile e il Dilettevole; red quilts, Irene Silvagni's collection. **36**: Nicoletta Marazza's house in Ramatuelle; tiles mosaic, Nicoletta Marazza design; glasses, Conran shop; iron stool, Claudia Pellegatta antique shop; curly iron tray, L'Utile e il Dilettevole. **37**: Nicoletta Marazza's house in Ramatuelle; turquoise awning, L'Utile e il Dilettevole. **38**: a Soho rooftop, New York; straw mat, L'Utile e il Dilettevole; red pillow & Japanese sandals, Pearl River; black tray, black teapot & bowl, Anthropologie; black handbinded book, Adalberto Cremonesi, Milan. **39**: architect's house in London designed by Dale Loth Architects, London; sarong & silk quilt, L'Utile e il Dilettevole; bamboo pole, Habitat; paper lanterns, L'Utile e il Dilettevole. **40 & 41**: La Bastide Rose, Nicole & Pierre Salinger's house at Le Thor, Provence; chair, Habitat; zinc basin & pitcher & linen towel, L'Utile e il Dilettevole; pareo & night dress, Carla Saibene. **42**: see page 3. **43**: **l** silk organza shoulder bag, L'Utile e il Dilettevole; **r** deckchair, Habitat; towel, Les Galeries Tropeziennes; flask, La Compagnia Coloniale. **44 & 45**: folding cot, folding stool, pillow, & awning, L'Utile e il Dilettevole. **48 & 49**: Giorgio & Irene Silvagni's house in Provence; iron bed by Giorgio Silvagni at L'Utile e il Dilettevole; Moroccan plaid, embroidered bag, & slippers, Compagnia dell'Oriente; silk moiré pillow, L'Utile e il Dilettevole. **50 & 51**: Enrica Stabile's house, Le Thor, Provence; old shower basin, Flore Derenne, L'Isle sur la Sorgue. **52**: La Bastide Rose, Nicole & Pierre Salinger's house, Le Thor, Provence; bathing accessories, Coté Bastide; chair, Habitat; enamelled basin & pitcher & linen towel, L'Utile e il Dilettevole. **53**: **l** La Bastide Rose, Nicole & Pierre Salinger's house, Le Thor, Provence; sarong & linen dress, Carla Saibene; **r** Enrica Stabile's house, Le Thor, Provence. **54 & 55**: Juju Restaurant, Beaduc beach, Camargue. **56**: Enrica Stabile's house, Le Thor, Provence; gauze tablecloth & chair covers & antique lanterns, L'Utile e il Dilettevole. **57**: Enrica Stabile's house, Le Thor, Provence; **l** blue glass pitcher, L'Utile e il Dilettevole; **r** gauze chair covers & green plate, L'Utile e il Dilettevole. **58**: Mr & Mrs Degrugillier, Le Mas de Flore, Antiquite et Creation, Lagnes, Isle sur Sorgue, Provence; wooden gazebo by order Le Mas de Flore. **59**: Mr & Mrs Degrugillier, Le Mas de Flore, Antiquite et Creation, Lagnes, Isle sur Sorgue, Provence; patchwork tablecloth, tea service & plates, L'Utile e il Dilettevole. **60**: Enrica Stabile's house, Le Thor, Provence; teacup & pillow, L'Utile e il Dilettevole. **61**: Enrica Stabile's house, Le Thor, Provence; tablecloth, pillows, & teacup, L'Utile e il Dilettevole. **62**: Enrica Stabile's house, Le Thor, Provence; **l** table & mosquito net, Les Jardins de Provence; glasses & plates, L'Utile e il Dilettevole; **r** tray & glasses, Habitat. **63**: Enrica Stabile's house, Le Thor, Provence; lanterns, Habitat;

glasses, L'Utile e il Dilettevole. **64 & 65**: Thank you to Juliette, Paul & Romeo de Menthon. **68**: glasses & flatware, Les Galeries Tropeziennes. **69**: plates & glasses, Les Galeries Tropeziennes. **70**: tablecloth, L'Utile e il Dilettevole. **71**: pitcher, glasses, & tablecloth, L'Utile e il Dilettevole; plates & cutlery, Habitat. **72**: Giorgio Irene Silvagni's house in Provence; African cloth, Galerie Afrique Ramatuelle. **73**: Giorgio Irene Silvagni's house in Provence; straw blinds, Les Jardins de Provence; African textiles, Galerie Afrique Ramatuelle. **74**: Giorgio Irene Silvagni's house in Provence; wire 'presentoir,' L'Utile e il Dilettevole; green pottery, Irene Silvagni's collection. **75**: Giorgio Irene Silvagni's house in Provence. **76**: **l** enamel plates & bowl, L'Utile e il Dilettevole; **r** bolster, pillow, & satin shoulder bag, l'Utile e il Dilettevole. **77**: tea caddy, shoulder bag, plates, chopsticks, & bowls, l'Utile e il Dilettevole. **78**: a house in New York; **l** tablecloth & pillows, l'Utile e il Dilettevole; **tr** golden bowls, Anthropologie; **br** pillow, l'Utile e il Dilettevole. **79**: **l** golden bowls, Anthropologie; **r** Chinese paper lantern, L'Utile e il Dilettevole. **80 & 81**: garden designer Mary Z. Jenkins's house in New York; table mats, pitcher, glasses, plates, bowls, & flatware, White on White; barbecue tools, Crate and Barrel. **82**: garden designer Mary Z. Jenkins's house in New York; **t** barbecue tools, Crate and Barrel; **b** candles bags holders, White on White; wire baskets, salad bowls, glasses, plates, & flasks, Crate and Barrel. **83**: a Soho roof top New York; tablecloth, l'Utile e il Dilettevole; plates, bowls, apron, & dishtowel, White on White; barbecue & tools, Crate and Barrel. **84 & 85**: screen, pillow, tablecloth, towels, & baskets, l'Utile e il Dilettevole; food box & plates, La Compagnia Coloniale. **86**: **l** wire basket & plates, l'Utile e il Dilettevole; towel, Conran Shop; glasses, Habitat; **tr** chair, basket, towels, & flask, L'Utile e il Dilettevole. **88 & 89**: Guido & Marilea Somaré's house in Milan; wicker armchair, l'Utile e il Dilettevole. **90 & 91**: a roof terrace in New York. **92 & 93**: Mrs Capron's garden in London; trug basket, garden tools, clogs, & canvas bag, Garden Images. **94 & 95**: Enrica Stabile's house, Le Thor, Provence; green flowers vases & china cache pot, l'Utile e il Dilettevole. **96 &**

97: Mr & Mrs Degrugillier, Le Mas de Flore, Antiquite et Creation, Lagnes, Isle sur Sorgue, Provence; garden table & chair, Le Mas de Flore; pillow, l'Utile e il Dilettevole. **96**: **b** Enrica Stabile's house, Le Thor, Provence; garden bench, pillows, watering can, tea cup, & basket, l'Utile e il Dilettevole. **98**: La Bastide Rose, Nicole & Pierre Salinger's house, Le Thor, Provence; baskets & pillow, L'Utile e il Dilettevole. **99 & 100**: Guido & Marilea Somaré's house in Milan; garden chair, l'Utile e il Dilettevole. **101**: garden designer Mary Z. Jenkins's house in New York. **102 & 103**: Mr & Mrs Degrugillier, Le Mas de Flore, Antiquite et Creation, Lagnes, Isle sur Sorgue, Provence; bird house & garden furniture, Le Mas de Flore; bird house & garden table, Le Mas de Flore. **104**: **tl** chairs, Habitat; **bl** deckchairs, beach umbrella, Claude Vacherot; **r** Sailor's canvas chair, Habitat. **105**: **tl** La Bastide Rose, Nicole & Pierre Salinger's house, Le Thor, Provence; garden chair & tin candleholder, l'Utile e il Dilettevole; blue bag, Minh Mang; glass, Habitat; **tr** Enrica Stabile's house, Le Thor, Provence; glasses, pitchers, & wire basket, l'Utile e il Dilettevole; **br** deckchair, pillows, & tray, l'Utile e il Dilettevole; blue glasses, Habitat. **106**: **tl** a Soho roof terrace, New York; glasses & bolster, Anthropologie; **tr** architect's house in London designed by Dale Loth Architects, London; teck garden bench, Habitat, pillow, l'Utile e il Dilettevole; **br** Siegliende Wondert's terrace in Milan. **107**: **l** architect's house in London designed by Dale Loth Architects, London; **r** Joanna Saunders's house in London; egg garden chair & cane poles, Habitat. **108**: Mrs Capron's garden in London; garden chair & pillow, l'Utile e il Dilettevole. **109**: **l** Mrs Capron's garden in London; pillows, l'Utile e il Dilettevole; **r** Enrica Stabile's house, Le Thor, Provence; pillow, l'Utile e il Dilettevole. **110**: **l** baby shoes, La Compagnia dell'Oriente; bolster, Anthropologie; **r** pillow, l'Utile e il Dilettevole. **111**: Joanna Saunders's house in London; pillows, napkin, pitcher, & curtain, l'Utile e il Dilettevole. **112**: garden designer Mary Z. Jenkins' house in New York; pillows, White on White. **113**: **r** a terrace in New York; pillow, l'Utile e il Dilettevole. **114**: Joanna Saunders' house in London; hurricane lamps & pitcher, l'Utile e il Dilettevole. **115**: Guido &

Marilea Somarè's house in Milan; bamboo garden lamps Habitat. **116**: Siegliende Wondert's house in Milan; hurricane lantern, white embroidered lamp, l'Utile e il Dilettevole. **117**: **l** Joel & Yuta Powell's house in the Hudson River Valley; **r** antique lanterns l'Utile e il Dilettevole. **118**: **l** Joanna Saunders' house in London; Chinese lantern l'Utile e il Dilettevole; bamboo poles Habitat; **r** garden designer Mary Z. Jenkins' house in New York; garden light White on White. **119**: **l** Nicoletta Marazza's house, Ramatuelle; curtain l'Utile e il Dilettevole; **r** table mat, glasses, lantern Anthropologie. **138**: a rooftop in New York; bathroom accessories Crate and Barrel. **140**: **t** rooftop in New York; lanterns, Moroccan glasses Anthropologie.

index

Figures in *italics* refer to captions; those in **bold** refer to projects.

acknowledgments

I'm a city dweller by necessity and not by choice. My escape is to browse through books and magazines dreaming of a different lifestyle—healthier, greener and in touch with nature. I dream in technicolor. So I was thrilled and excited when Gabriella Le Grazie for RPS offered me rather unexpectedly the chance to make other people share my dream. So first of all I wish to thank Gabriella for her continuous encouragement and professional advise; a true friend all the way. Also big thanks to Alice Berkeley and Chris Drake. Alice, the best of friends, shared with me all the work and some good laughs. Without her there would not have been such knowledgeable text. Chris, I simply couldn't have had a better photographer to work with: totally committed, extremely patient, and always good humored. There are no words, he is simply the best. A special thank to my daughter Carlotta and to Alberto Bellinzona, who shared, as very capable assistants, the most difficult part of the job. A very big thank you to Gail Cook, Mary Walker, Bette Weed, and Rina Schafman, and to all my team and friends of l'Utile e il Dilettevole who did wonders to help me in many ways. And thank you to my mother who spent a long time helping me to find the right words to put it all into captions. Thank you to Alison Starling, to Sophie Bevan, and to Catherine Randy for their professional involvement and for actually making the book come true in pages and chapters. And last but not least, thank you to Franco my husband, who carried, built, drove, and cooked. I could have not asked for more!

Thank you most warmly to all the friends who shared with me their lovely yards, patios, terraces, roof tops; it was very hard work but a wonderful experience!